A CUP OF COMFORT®

for

BREAST CANCER SURVIVORS

Inspiring stories of
courage and triumph

Edited by Colleen Sell

adamsmedia
Avon, Massachusetts

In loving memory of Deborah St. Denis

A Cup of Comfort® is a registered trademark of F+W Publications, Inc.

Published by
Adams Media, an F+W Publications Company
57 Littlefield Street, Avon, MA 02322 U.S.A.
www.adamsmedia.com and *www.cupofcomfort.com*

ISBN-10: 1-60550-644-3
ISBN-13: 978-1-60550-644-9

Printed in the United States of America.

J I H G F E D C B A

Library of Congress Cataloging-in-Publication Data
is available from the publisher.

This publication is designed to provide accurate and authoritative information with regard to the subject matter covered. It is sold with the
understanding that the publisher is not engaged in rendering legal,
accounting, or other professional advice. If legal advice or other expert
assistance is required, the services of a competent professional person
should be sought.

—From a *Declaration of Principles* jointly adopted by
a Committee of the American Bar Association and
a Committee of Publishers and Associations

Many of the designations used by manufacturers and sellers to distin-
guish their products are claimed as trademarks. Where those designations appear in this book and Adams Media was aware of a trademark
claim, the designations have been printed with initial capital letters.

This book is available at quantity discounts for bulk purchases.
For information, please call 1-800-289-0963.

Contents

Foreword vi

Introduction • Colleen Sell. viii

Inga • Lauren Reece Flaum. 1

My Third Lung • Laura Walsh Plunkett. 7

The Friend Who Came and Went • Sheryl Kraft 16

Code Red • Nikki Marchesiello 25

Warrior Women Wear Pink • Christy Caballero 33

Letter 7 • Karen A. Condon. 42

Probably Nothing • Harriett Ford. 47

Carrying My Head in a Nordstrom's Bag •

    Jennifer S. Kutzik 56

In the Eye of the Sparrow • Anya Silver. 63

Survival of the Fittest • Linda Holland Rathkopf 72

Lessons from the Chemo Room • Stacia Deutsch 80

Dear Tumor • Julie A. Whitney 87

Filling Up and Spilling Over • Kathie Ragsdale. 96

Led by Love • Susan B. Townsend 102

The "M" Word • Joseph Pantatello. 108

Only My Sisters Understand • Cathy Howard 104

Proceed • Mary Ann O'Rourke. 119

Remember Only the Laughter • Margaret B. Davidson . . 126

Pieta's Promise • Virginia Hardee Silverman 131

Hidden Treasures • Alice Muschany. 137

Location, Location, Location • Sally Gilchrest-Unrau. . . .141

Well Wishes • Jennifer Swanson. 149

I Went and Washed That Hair Right Offa My Head •

    Maria S. Judge. 154

Good to Go • Annette M. Bower.................. 162

Before and After • Jeanne Schambra 168

The Luckiest Family on the Block • Beth Gooch 165

Staying Afloat • Caroline Castle Hicks 182

Mind Over Cancer • Kate Kenworthy 188

The Pebble and the Rock: A Love Story •

    Rosalie Marsh-Boinus........................ 196

Saving Grace • Paula Sword 204

There's No Place Like Normal • Jennifer D. Jenkins 211

Surviving Period • Rachel Beth McClain.............216

The Challenge • Petrina Aubol 221

From To-Do to Ta-Da! • Kathleen Griswold.......... 230

Missing Parts • Glen Finland 235

Timing Is Everything • Joan A. Cody............... 244

Never Say Never • Allison Jean Roberts 253

Dancing in the Moonlight • C. Lynn Beck 260

Breast Cancer, Funny? • Barbara Leedom............ 267

Bonus Time • Michele Ivy Davis................... 273

The Hoopla about Hair • Beth Dotson Brown........ 279

Daffodils and Me • Ruth Ellen Weiner.............. 287

A Breast Party • Donna Conrad................... 294

The Power of Knowledge • Janine Boldrin........... 300

Go Ahead and Wish for It • Sheila O'Brien Schimpf ... 306

Like a Rock • Claudia Sternbach 313

Contributors......................................316

Acknowledgments

Never have I felt more indebted to the collaborators of any book than I do to the authors whose stories grace these pages. Not only did they contribute powerful stories about their personal experiences with breast cancer, they did so amiably and professionally, making my job of selecting, compiling, and editing this book both a pleasure and an honor.

Thanks go to my top-notch collaborators at Adams Media—Meredith O'Hayre, project editor; Paula Munier, director of innovation; Laura Daly, senior project manager; and Jacquinn Williams, publicist—as well as to the book's eagle-eyed copyeditor, Carol Goff.

As always, I am grateful to my *seanchaithe* ancestors for passing along their storytelling genes and to my family for enabling me to do the work I love.

Foreword

When her grandmother died of breast cancer, Andrea Thomas Hill knew she wanted to take action to raise funds and awareness for the disease. In particular, she was saddened by the fact that her grandmother had been too ashamed of her disease to talk about her experience. Inspired by a breast cancer fundraising race in the United States, Andrea organized the first-ever Canadian Breast Cancer Foundation run for breast cancer.

The first run took place in Toronto's High Park in 1992 with 800 participants who raised an amazing $85,000 for the cause. In 2007, the Canadian Breast Cancer Foundation CIBC Run for the Cure took place in fifty-three communities across Canada, and 170,000 participants raised over $27 million for breast cancer research.

Established in 1986 by a dedicated group of volunteers, the Canadian Breast Cancer Foundation is the leading national volunteer-based organization in Canada dedicated to creating a future without breast cancer. Since 1992, through the passionate and generous support of individuals and organizations that share our vision, the Foundation has invested more than $120 million in relevant and innovative breast cancer research and effective community initiatives.

With support from our donors, our corporate partners, and events like the Run, we continue investing in our vision of creating a future without breast cancer. In working toward our goal, we look for inspiration in the lives of survivors and their families, some of whom have shared their stories in this book. They are stories of strength, courage, and hope. We hope you will be as inspired by their stories as we are.

The stories in this book are not meant to provide medical information. If you have any questions about breast cancer or its treatment, you are encouraged to consult a health care professional. To learn more about the work of the Canadian Breast Cancer Foundation, breast cancer, or breast health, visit *www.cbcf.org* or call 1-800-387-9816.

Introduction

"Cancer makes a woman out of you. After that you become a warrior. Survival is not so much about the body, but rather it is about the triumph of the human spirit."

—Danita Vance

One in eight.

I think of the women in my immediate family and wonder, will it be Mom, Nita, Linney, Jennifer, Christie, Grace, Stacey, or Jessica? I think of close friends and wonder, will it be Judy, Ellen, Sherri, Kelley, Indi, Barb, Paula, or Mardeene? Will it be me? Will two of us be among the one in eight women in the United States who will develop breast cancer at some point in their lives? If so, I hope we are among the increasing number of breast cancer survivors, which currently stands at about 2.5 million. And I hope we face the disease and live our lives with the same courage, strength, humor, hope, integrity, dignity, authenticity, and grace of the forty-five women whose stories appear in this book.

One in *eight.*

That's 12 percent of the adult female population of the United States. This year alone, more than 260,000 American women will be diagnosed with breast cancer, about 75 percent of which will be invasive forms of the disease. Our sisters to the north, in Canada, aren't faring much better. In fact, North America has the highest rate of breast cancer in the world. And let's not forget our sisters around the globe; breast cancer is on the rise worldwide. So, while breast cancer awareness, early detection, decreased use of hormone replacement therapy, healthier lifestyles, and more effective cancer treatments are improving survival rates, breast cancer is still one of the most prevalent and serious diseases afflicting women today. And it takes the lives of 46,000 American women each year.

One in **eight**.

I wonder, will the risk be less by the time my sixteen-year-old niece, Danielle, and my twelve-year-old granddaughter, Brianna, reach maturity? Will the rate of breast cancer incidence continue to decrease while the rate of survival continues to increase, as they have the past few years? Will there be a cure within Dani's and Nani's lifetimes? I hope so. I believe so.

And organizations like Susan G. Komen for the Cure® are working hard to make it so. So are myriad corporations and millions of individuals from all walks of life—many of whom are breast cancer survivors, women living with breast cancer, and their loved ones. Together, working with heart and smarts and chutzpah, a cure will be found. Lives will be saved, and lives will be improved. That's why the publisher of this book, Adams Media, has made a $5,000 donation to Susan G. Komen for the Cure® on behalf of Susan Reece Flaum, the author whose story, "Inga," opens this collection.

All forty-six stories in A Cup of Comfort® for Breast Cancer Survivors speak not only to the survival of these warrior women but also to the triumph of their spirits. I hope their stories will comfort and inspire you.

—Colleen Sell

Inga

I played a little game with Inga's face—well, her chin mostly, her deep, plunging chin that reminded me of an icicle with its tip snapped abruptly off. I'd never seen another chin like it; it was more a caricature than a real feature. And I had nothing but time to study it, watching her enter and exit my room, sometimes with a Styrofoam cup of chicken noodle soup, sometimes with a printout of the day's blood counts, all too often with thick plastic bags of toxic fluids targeting my tired veins. Each time she was in my presence, I'd seek out that odd triangular shape and in its recognition know that, somehow, Inga would yet again get me through the difficult day ahead.

The little game involved finding this same slightly askew triangle in the patterns that adorned Inga's clothing, in the vee of her wrap-style nursing smock, in the turquoise stones of her bracelet, in the spaces created on her feet by the crisscrosses of her sturdy shoes. I don't know if she knew she had a triangular theme going, or if it was some deep unconscious reiteration of what she saw when she looked in the mirror each morning getting ready for her hard day's work as head nurse in the chemotherapy suite. For me, scrutinizing Inga and her chin and her crazy triangular patterning became a ritual. The triangles kept recurring—in her cheekbones and her barrettes and the creases of her eyelids—and finding them never failed to bring me a surprising measure of comfort.

I've been in and out of the chemotherapy suite for twelve years now. Besides the nurses and the aides and the volunteer coffee ladies, I'm the rare person that continues to call the chemo suite my home away from home. Twelve years in and out of those antiseptic doors, rounds and rounds of drugs whose lists of just the side-effects take the nurses fifteen minutes to recite: nausea, vomiting, hair loss, skin changes, headache, diarrhea, fever, chills, bruising, achy bones, itchy skin, toe fungus, shortness of breath, blurred vision, compromised motor control, loss of appetite, not to mention the swift and premature departure of any sense of personal well-being and peace of mind. And that's supposed to be the good news, the things that happen when the chemo is working.

But Inga, always Inga, made it better. Each Thursday she reserved my favorite bed by the window with the view of the gray parking ramp and the grayer Iowa skies. She padded into and out of the room in hushed tones. She spoke descriptively in a soothing whisper. And she spoke only when necessary. Inga didn't laugh at me the time I brought in a stack of bills to pay during chemo. And she didn't bat an eye when I couldn't even hold the pen between my fingers when signing the first check and she was left to gather the tumbled bills at my bedside. She didn't panic—like her colleagues did—the time the tubing unhinged from the IV pump while I was asleep, and blood and chemo fluid flooded the floor. I'll never forget waking up to a half dozen nurses dressed in garments like from Three Mile Island cleaning up the spill!

Inga was the mother of two—older daughter, younger son—just like me, and her two were a couple of years ahead of mine in school. During the summers, when I would leave my kids home alone so I could go get the chemo, she would leave hers home alone so she could give it to me. We would laugh together, musing at the state the house would be in at the end of the day: chores undone, empty pizza boxes open on the countertop, the potential of a summer's day squandered in front of the squawking TV. Beneath my laughter, I'd envy the sense of security her children had—their mother heading out in the morning in nursing scrubs and sensible shoes, strong and ready to help people suffering from cancer—versus the insecurity my children were dealt, their mother sick with cancer, coming home sicker from treatment. I envied that truth of Inga's life, along with all that I admired in her cool competence, her quiet authority, and her deep, calming heart. Mostly, I envied Inga and her family that feeling of everyday life . . . before becoming aware of its tragic unfolding in one's own backyard.

Occasionally, I would bring small gifts to Inga—moisturizing cream for her healing hands, a linzertorte I baked. I'd write her notes about what she'd taught me about illness—its sanctity, its otherness, its necessity as a third urgent presence between life and death.

Inga became a sort of muse to me. When I started writing, I wrote about Inga. I imagined her to be a gardener of root vegetables—beets and onions and carrots and rutabaga—goodness planted so deep it would stoically endure the harsh Iowa winters, so deep her hardy hands would be thick with soil when digging in spring. I imagined her loving her solitude and her family in equal measures. I imagined her in prayer. She could have been a nun.

It was in the spring of 2005, when I was climbing out of the depths of chemotherapy, that I heard that

Inga was sick. She'd stopped coming into work. She was on disability. Inga, cancer's caretaker, was stricken with cancer—a rare cancer of the tongue with a poor prognosis. I wrote to her that day: Inga, how could it be? But Inga's disease was fast and vicious. I never heard back. She soon lost the ability to speak, then to eat, and within a year she lost her beautiful life.

This past autumn, the nurses and doctors in the cancer center dedicated a painting of a nurse to hang in the chemo suite in Inga's honor. They invited me to attend the ceremony and to read the letter I'd written in praise of Inga that had been published in the local newspaper. The event was held in a back room of the cancer center, a room I'd passed a hundred times when it was buzzing with physicians in white coats, peering at scans and tumors and pictures of luminous bones on light boxes. This day, it was laid out with cheese and crackers and a lime-green sherbet punch that looked a little too much like a chemo agent for my taste.

I was the only patient in the room amongst a sea of faces who had saved my life over and over during the last twelve years. But there was one face in that room that stood out. And it stood out at the chin. Inga's daughter, Susan, was at the far end of the room, standing between her father and her brother. They were both leaning on her, heads inclined toward that deep narrow chin, like an icicle with the tip snapped abruptly off. *The daughter is a replica of the mother,* I thought to myself, her complexion as soft, her strength as apparent, her movement as graceful. And sure enough, before I even realized what I was doing, I sought and found in her boots and her bag and her jewelry a series of elongated misshapen triangles.

I read my letter about Inga, about how her dignity made an unforgettable difference in the life of a patient. Reading the words, I worked really hard to hold back my tears so that everything wouldn't become a blur. I couldn't stand to miss a moment of watching Inga's unparalleled brand of comfort still, apparently, so hard at work.

—*Lauren Reece Flaum*

My Third Lung

I heard a brisk knock on the door, and my new physician entered the room with a confident stride. As I lay on the bed, I couldn't help but glance at her. I had to admit she was adorable. I was skeptical of most doctors at that point, but this one was hard not to like. She was blonde with shoulder-length curly hair and a petite frame. She said hello as she carefully placed her two medical kits at the foot of my bed, then came over to shake my hand.

She introduced herself and explained that she would need to perform an exam. I told her I had many doctors who had been poking at me every day. This was not a lie. I had been stripped of modesty long ago with the excessive monitoring of doctors, medical students, nurses, and other health professionals. It was getting old. But my new doctor crossed her arms and looked through me with intensity.

As if her piercing blue eyes weren't convincing enough, she then placed her delicate hands on the right side of my ribs. She knew where the pain was, where my heartache lay. She was tender, empathetic. I would not deny her this exam. It was important to both of us. She was my daughter, Morgan. She was six, just trying to cope with my latest bout with breast cancer.

I had been diagnosed two-and-a-half years before; invasive ductal carcinoma was the name for my disease. After finding the lump on my left breast, I'd been swift in getting to a doctor and pragmatic in my treatment approach. My husband, Michael, and I established a thorough medical team and began a plan of attack immediately. My primary tumor was so small that doctors predicted I probably wouldn't have any other tumors elsewhere in the body. I was skeptical, as this was all based on normalized data; I was not a statistic. My instinct proved cruelly prophetic; we soon learned that a small tumor had already formed on a lymph node closest to the left breast and another on my liver.

Cancer is a deceptive enemy; it can overwhelm the immune system. In a healthy body, the good cells can identify and kill the bad cells so that cancer doesn't grow. In my case, my immune system got confused and started to grow the cancer cells. No one knows why I got cancer; even the most educated physicians can't tell me why I got this disease. They can only tell me what fed my cancer, what made it grow.

Breast cancer is typically fueled by the hormones estrogen or progesterone, or a protein called "her-2-neu." Those are the known catalysts; there also can be numerous unknown factors that trigger growth. Cancer is still a mystery, even to the experts. My cancer was fueled by "her-2," as it is called. This is the more aggressive form of breast cancer.

When I first got diagnosed, Michael and I got the pathology report in a piecemeal fashion. The only constant in the multitude of information we received was that my disease was aggressive. Yet, my diagnosis came at an optimal time, when modern technology was beginning to catch up with my type of cancer. Herceptin and other medicines were making headway in the fight.

As Morgan went back to gather her equipment, I contemplated the turmoil that had interrupted our lives only a month before when we learned the breast cancer had returned. This time, it had spread to the lung and was encapsulated in two oblong tumors, one in the upper lobe and one in the middle lobe of my right lung. Both of the tumors were small and operable, as before. I was grateful to have this as an option.

It had been eighteen months since our last episode of cancer, during which my chronic condition had been considered "stable" the whole time. Since I was stage IV from the beginning, I would never be deemed "cured" by the medical industry. Stable was the best grade I could receive in this classroom. I learned to accept it, and once acclimated, I discovered there is much living I can do. Once my family and I had recovered from the twenty rounds of hard-hitting chemotherapy, we resumed normal life. We kept moving forward with the hope that our toxic approach to the disease would be enough for us to move on with regular life afterward. My hair started to grow back, and I worked on restoring my energy. I began cycling for sport, which helped me to develop my strength, both mental and physical. Little did I know that it would help to make my surgical recovery more tolerable. I was constantly conditioning myself for life, and in turn, the next step against cancer.

Michael and I had always involved the children in every part of our family; we tried to recognize them as little people. Morgan was four years old when I got diagnosed; Jack was ten months old. There was little we could tell Jack as an infant, but with Morgan, we needed to make her aware of the process ahead. Before my mastectomy, Michael took her out for a drive and told her about Mommy having a bad spot that doctors would need to get out. He explained that I wouldn't feel well, that she would see me in the hospital.

When I lost my hair, Michael and I had the children there when we shaved my head. We let them touch my prickly scalp. We even told them they could make a wish if they put a hand on my head. We laughed with them; it felt good to laugh about my disease. We wanted them to know it was okay, that I would be fine. When I went through the chemotherapy with intravenous infusion, the kids would sometimes come to treatment. They knew all the nurses and physicians and felt comfortable in that environment. It was important to both Michael and me that the kids be empathetic to those who were sick, whether it was our family or someone else's.

So it came as no surprise to me that Morgan would need to use medical play in order to heal her emotions with my lung surgery. While I was restoring my lungs, she was mending her heart. I was proud of her for letting herself feel the emotion, for wanting to play a role in my recovery. It was healthy, and I would indulge her. Morgan's plastic tools included stethoscopes, a thermometer, blood pressure cuff, and a scalpel.

Morgan also added my breathing tools, two spirometers that I had received from the hospital, to add legitimacy to her exam. She and Jack had seen the respiratory care specialists help me to use the spirometers to gauge my breathing and recovery. The kids actually fought over the meters while I was in the hospital. One helped me inhale, the other to exhale. We took the tools from the hospital more as souvenirs than anything else, reminders that I could breathe again after the surgery.

Morgan put her ill-fitting stethoscope around her neck and came back over to the right side of the bed. It was the bed I'd slept in through high school, in what had once been my bedroom but was now a guest room. We were at my parents' home during the day so I could take the appropriate pain medicines and they could help with the kids. Though I was relatively sleepy from the meds, I remember Morgan's exam in detail. She used the plastic stethoscope to measure my breathing. She said she heard the "bumping" of my heart, that there was a problem with it. She thought surgery was necessary, her way of being part of the decision process.

Morgan then grabbed the remedial blood pressure cuff and placed it around my arm. It was small and would not fit around my upper arm, but I let her put it around my lower arm. The machine was broken, but we faked our way through that part. We both decided my blood pressure was normal; I've always had relatively low blood pressure, so it seemed acceptable to short-change this part of the exam.

She took my temperature and decided I had a fever. She, once again, mumbled that surgery would seem to be the best option. I agreed with her conclusion. She gathered the orange scalpel and began to do her work on my right side, where she knew I was recovering. She was still careful; she knew my ribs were sore from the actual recovery. The chest tubes had caused bruising on my ribs, which was one of the reasons I still took the pain medication.

She then put down her scalpel and began to massage the general area, gently. My sweet and tender little girl was adding alternative medicine to her procedure. After thirty seconds, she looked at me in a resolute fashion.

"It's done," she said. "I took out your third lung."

I was not sure what she meant, although I had a trace of an idea. I looked at her inquisitively and asked her to explain. I didn't want to force her answers with any leading questions. She sighed, and went on to tell me she'd overheard my sister, Heather, talking to someone on the phone when I was in the hospital. She said Heather had told the caller that I was doing well but was tired after having my "third lung" removed.

During the actual surgery, my doctor and his team cut through the latissimus muscle in my back, broke a rib, deflated my right lung, and tested lymph tissue near the lung before accessing the tumors. Though the focus of the surgery was to remove the tumors from the upper lobe and middle lobe, the surgeon thought the tissue on the lower lobe was suspicious for cancer. So he removed it as a precautionary measure. This lobe represents one of three lobes on the right lung, or one-third. This is where Morgan got her wording askew—"third lung" versus "one-third" of a lung. Both my "third lung" and the lymph nodes had no cancer in them, "no evidence of disease" as the pathology report reads.

Morgan asked if I felt better. I said "yes," and she went on playing with her doctor equipment for a bit. I was stunned at my daughter's awareness. In her own terms, she understood. She knew parts of me had been removed and life would go back to a new normal, similar to but different than before. She knew the sickness had gotten to my lungs but that it didn't compromise the quality of our daily life. I was still here, fighting, as I would continue to do with modern medicines as potent weapons in my arsenal. But now I realized that my daughter was fighting with me.

What a brave little soldier she was, too. At six, Morgan already understood a reality I was just coming to terms with—that cancer had taken something from me I didn't need and given me something I hadn't known I wanted. Though I'd lost my "third" lung, I'd gained the gift of my child's awakening. Morgan's ability to understand and to accept our situation breathed new life into me, and has done so every day since. That was more fresh air than my lung tissue could give me.

I got up from the bed, and Morgan came to join me. Hand in hand, we walked out of the bedroom, leaving our fears behind, following our hearts toward the future.

—*Laura Walsh Plunkett*

The Friend Who Came and Went

We loved each other immediately. It was an unexpected love, as deep as it was sudden. Meeting in our thirties, we were brought together by an illness we shared, an illness that only one of us survived.

A well-meaning woman from the breast cancer support group at the Greenwich YWCA had slipped Shelley my phone number one night, the night that I, unfulfilled, decided not to return to the group. "Here," the woman had said to Shelley, "call her. She's young, like you." Maybe it shouldn't have been true, but as a thirty-four-year-old mother of two toddlers, I felt no bond with the rest of the group, older women who seemed to accept their illness with a resignation that I, in the prime of life and feeling blind-sided by fate, could not begin to summon.

Shelley and I talked on the phone for hours, making a date to meet in person the next night. We were blown away by how much, besides breast cancer, we had in common. We lived about 20 minutes from one another. Her daughter and my oldest son had been born just one month apart. We were both Jewish. We both loved shopping, movies, and eating out. And we were both feeling isolated and alone with our fear. When we first spotted each another in front of the Boxing Cat Grill, we hugged without self-consciousness, like old friends reunited after a long absence. We sat in the crowded restaurant, deaf to the hubbub around us, lost in our mutual discovery of a soul mate.

Shelley was my drink of water after a long thirst. A great sense of relief coursed through my body. After I ordered, Shelley told the waiter, "I'll have what she's having." Although we both loved eating salmon, brown rice, and healthy green salads, our plates sat untouched for hours, our mouths too busy talking to eat, the steam from our food long dissolved into the vapor of our chitchat.

We liked so many of the same things. We were both crazy about long dangling earrings, cowboy boots, and sunglasses in all shapes and colors. We both loved coffee frozen yogurt, snacking on sunflower seeds between meals, and bagels with their middles gouged out. We both sighed over George Clooney, the movie *The English Patient*, and Alice Hoffman's books.

After sharing the most intimate details about our childhoods, our families, and our careers, how comforting it was to realize that there was no need for me to explain why, since my diagnosis, I'd awaken in the middle of the night paralyzed with dread, my head throbbing with unanswerable "what-ifs." *What if the cancer comes back? What if my children have to grow up without a mother? What if the pain is unbearable?* Nor did Shelley have to explain why, weeks before each visit to her oncologist, she'd lose her appetite and drop five pounds.

"Wanna see my scar?" she asked suddenly.

"I'll show you mine if you show me yours," I answered.

We jumped up from the dinner table, sending the silverware tumbling to the floor, and practically ran to the restroom at the back of the restaurant. Giddy from the red wine we'd gulped down on empty stomachs, giggling like schoolgirls, we crowded into a tiny stall. There, we lifted up our shirts, pulled down our bras, and stared at the mirror images of our own mastectomy scars. Shelley had lost her right breast five years earlier; I'd lost my left breast just four months before that night, four days before Christmas. The night I'd come home from the hospital, neighborhood carolers gathered below my bedroom window, with no clue that inside I lay under piles of blankets, weeping at the sheer unfairness of life.

Shelley stared. Another person might have looked, drawn in her breath, and uttered something like, "Oh, well, it's not so bad," and then quickly averted her eyes. But knowing how much we had suffered to get here, each of us also knew that our scars deserved more than a fleeting glance. Carved deep into our chests to preserve our lives, these emblems of a so-far-successful battle against a terrible adversary bound us together. At that moment, we were not only looking at one another's scars, we were also looking into one another's hearts.

No one except my husband, Alan, the doctors, and my mother had seen me naked since the surgery. In fact, even before I could look at myself, I had insisted that Alan look at me when I lay in my hospital bed the day after the operation. I leaned back on the rough pale sheets, giving myself completely to him like the first time we had made love. "Please look," I said, as I gently pulled the bandages aside. I stared hard into his eyes, searching for some kind of reaction, a response to my changed body. But his expression never changed. After a moment he moved the bandages back over my wound and refastened my hospital gown, then he kissed the top of my head reassuringly, without saying a word. It wasn't until a week later, in the privacy of my bathroom at home, that I worked up the nerve to face my naked body in the mirror. I bit my lip and stared, fighting hard not to cry out, and at that moment I realized that not only had my body been drastically altered, but I had been, too. I was enmeshed in a cacophony of feelings: although I had traded my breast for my survival, I immediately mourned my loss. I would never look, or be, the same again.

Friends, family, counselors—they all tried to help. But no one succeeded in finding the right words. Their pleas that I remain optimistic, that I focus on the survivors and not the victims of breast cancer, fell on deaf ears. What did optimism mean in the face of cancer? How randomly the disease struck, how arbitrarily the survivors were chosen, how uncertain the fate of even the "luckiest" of us. No one seemed to have a clue about the reality of living with cancer—until I met Shelley.

To say that we became best friends would be an understatement. It was more like the first flush of young love. We shared daily—and nightly—phone calls and saw one another two, three, or four times a week. It was never enough; we always wanted more. One blustery cold winter night, we walked out of a restaurant where we had lingered long after the other patrons had left, and in the almost-empty parking lot, we noticed that Shelley's car was running, a white plume of exhaust curling up into the frigid air. She had been so excited to see me when we arrived for our dinner that she had jumped out of her car without turning off the ignition.

Alan was astonished at our rapid and intense bonding. "You love your friend more than you love me," he'd say, only half kidding, as he saw me dressing carefully one night to meet Shelley for a movie.

"Of course I don't," I reassured him. "I just love her . . . differently."

When, well past midnight, I'd tiptoe in the door and gently kiss his sleeping face, he'd mutter, "What time is it?" with a tone I can only describe as loving exasperation.

How could I explain to him that finding someone who knew just what I was feeling, at my bravest moments and at my most terrified, was a source of comfort that nothing else, not even his love, could provide? It was as if I had been running and running—whether toward or away from something, I couldn't even tell—until, suddenly, with Shelley, I could catch my breath.

Then, the ground gave way beneath us. Shelley came down with a fever that hung on. At first, she ignored it, thinking it must be a virus. But then, while trying to unscrew a stubborn jar, she broke her wrist. A few weeks later, her ankle snapped when she stepped off the curb the wrong way. A run of bad luck? Osteoporosis? Maybe. But what about the fever that wouldn't go away?

All of this happened in the midst of a separation from her husband.

"Maybe it's all the stress that's running you down?" I asked her late one night when we sat on the terrace of my summer home on Fire Island, calmed by the sound of the distant waves. Although she was feeling ill, she had come with her daughter to visit me. We had looked forward all year to this visit—a ritual we had enjoyed each of the five summers since we'd met. The stars were startlingly bright that night, and I remember looking up and finding one and making a silent wish: *Please, oh please, let my friend be healthy.* And then, with a shudder, the unbidden thought: *What if the cancer is back?*

In the following weeks, I found myself turning into one of those people I had shied away from after my diagnosis, urging optimism, bravery, and cheer. "You'll be fine," I encouraged, when Shelley confessed to her fear that the cancer might be returning. "It's been ten years. I *know* you are a survivor."

The phone call came late one night. As clearly as I remember my first child's first words, I remember Shelley's: "The cancer. It's back."

The next morning I packed my things, leaving my husband and children behind at the beach, and came home to help my friend.

This brought me face to face with the "what-ifs" I had fought so desperately against. But if I had to choose between her comfort and mine, it was no contest. I held Shelley's hand as the doctor extracted spinal fluid with a needle large enough for an elephant. I flew to North Carolina for her bone marrow transplant and sat in the waiting room watching bald-headed wraithlike women float noiselessly down the corridors. Months later, I sat vigil at the hospital where my best friend lay attached to myriad tubes after she had begged the doctors to try anything, everything, to make her well. I shielded my tears from her by turning my head to look out the window, but when I could no longer keep them inside, I ran to the bathroom, shut myself in a stall, and collapsed in fierce sobs.

It poured furiously the day of Shelley's funeral. As my family and I left the cemetery in Paramus and drove north toward Connecticut on I-95, the rain slowed to a timid drizzle and an astonishing rainbow—like melted gemstones of jades, rubies, amethysts, corals, and sapphires—stretched like taffy across the sky in an elegant arched row.

Will I ever stop missing the friend who came and went? I cannot imagine it. Today, I mailed her daughter a gift for her upcoming birthday. Arielle, who looks just like her mother, is turning twenty-one. She's away at college, the same college as my younger son. They are good friends and see each other regularly. Love, I believe, is stronger than fate. The bond that Shelley and I forged all those years ago lives on into the next generation.

—Sheryl Kraft

Code Red

I like to make plans. I plan everything, and if I'm not planning, I'm making lists. I'm organized, I tell myself, not a control freak, thank you very much. So, when I'm diagnosed with breast cancer, of course I plan. I plan for my post-surgery recovery and, because the tumor is small, I anticipate and plan for radiation and tamoxifen. I don't plan for chemotherapy.

"Chemotherapy?" Am I screaming?

I look at Nino, my husband, his shock and surprise mirroring my own.

"Yes," my oncologist says. "Even though the tumor is only one millimeter, it's an invasive ductal cancer and aggressive. I strongly recommend chemotherapy, tamoxifen, and then a six-week course of radiation." She explains her recommendations in detail and answers our questions. Every curse word I know blasts through my brain.

At home, I struggle to regain my balance. I remind myself that I can do this. I've always handled the trials and tribulations in my life with one pure thought: *As long as my son is healthy and not in harm's way, I can deal with anything.*

I think about the destruction that the chemotherapy drugs will wreak on my body: death to healthy cells, debilitating nausea, hair loss, weight loss, weakness. Do I want to do this? No. No. Absolutely not. But I do want to live, and I don't want to take a chance with my life. So I plan for chemotherapy.

I will receive four treatments, one every two weeks. I start the second week of January. Happy New Year.

I act brave during the day. I do this for all the people around me, because I know it makes them unhappy if I act vulnerable and scared. At night, though, when it's silent and still, I let the warm tears flow from my eyes and trickle into my ears. Come morning, I'm brave again.

The day of my first chemotherapy treatment arrives. Blatant in my show of false courage, I gussy up. I put on the soft, red cashmere sweater I love so much, brush my long hair until it gleams, and paint my lips red with my favorite Chanel lipstick. I'm going in style.

Curious, I wonder how the chemo will affect me. *What will the drug look like? What will it feel like as it courses through my body? How sick will I be? When will I lose my hair? What will I look like? Will I lose those ten extra pounds?*

I'm about to get all the answers, and then some.

I strut my gorgeous self down the hallway until I come to the treatment room door. I pull myself up, shoulders back, head high. I look tall, strong, and spunky. I know where I'm shining the sunshine.

The nurse greets and directs me to a lounge chair. She covers me with a warm, soft blanket, nurtures and coos over me; I'm in heaven. I return her smiles, and we chuckle and joke together. It's a wonderful time. She pulls a tall contraption over to the chair and, hanging from it, is a plastic bag filled with a gorgeous jewel-red liquid. I love the color; it matches my lips and sweater.

"Your chemo cocktail," she says.

For something so deadly, it sure is beautiful.

I'm relaxed and comfortable. Looking around, I notice I'm the only patient in the large room. The nurse eases the needle into the top of my left hand and carefully anchors it down with tape.

"This will take about two hours, Nikki," she says. She adjusts the bag and leaves me alone in the room.

I feel the coldness of the drug move through my body. I don't warm up for eight weeks.

Did I mention I hate being sick to my stomach? I mean, I hate it over all the other stuff. I'll take the headache, the cuts and bruises, the aches and pains, but let's skip the upset stomach, okay? It hits me hard about six hours later. Drooping over the toilet bowl, I retch with dry heaves, and I'm clammy with sweat. My mouth tastes sour, and my body smells rank.

"Nino, give me one of those pills, the kind for nausea. Please." My voice is high-pitched; I'm in full-tilt whine.

The pills don't work. I'm in hell. Two days pass in nausea, vomit, and exhaustion. Then I feel better, and I return to normal. *I can do this,* I think to myself. *I am doing this.* I clean house, tend to family, and go to work.

I begin to lose weight. I notice the change in my hair; it feels like it will crumble and turn to powder if I roll it between my fingers. I immediately call my stylist, Judy.

After examining my hair, she recommends a close-cropped cut. "You won't be so traumatized when your hair starts falling out," she says.

Judy cuts and shapes until my long, auburn hair is an inch short all over my head. I like it; I feel lighter. And very cute. Cutting edge.

Within days, I see more scalp than hair and my cuteness ebbs. I decide against wearing the artfully tied scarves or normal-looking wigs to hide my balding. Instead, I opt for hats; they're quick and easy.

It takes four days to bounce back from the second treatment. The anti-nausea pills still don't work, and I'm on a rollercoaster of nausea and visits to the toilet bowl. I stay in bed. I want off this ride.

The mouth sores make it painful to eat and drink. Undernourished and dehydrated, my flesh hangs and my muscle tone softens and slackens. To make matters worse, I'm extremely constipated, which is uncomfortable, to be delicate.

"I quit," I announce to Nino after the second treatment.

"Quit what? Chemo? You can't quit; you might die."

"I'm going to quit, and I'm not going to die. I'm going to find a way to beat cancer without chemo," I say.

I pace the living room floor, back and forth, brainstorming, stretching my mind for ideas. The day turns into evening. Nothing, nada, zero. There's no way out. In disgust, I capitulate.

Two more treatments to go.

My head doesn't have a pretty shape, another fine humiliation. A friend gives me a temporary four-inch tattoo of a bright orange crouching tiger, which I slap on the left side of my naked noggin, just over my ear. That thing stays on for weeks, too, which is excellent.

No longer curious and eager when I walk into the treatment room, I'm sick before I reach the door. I'm a slobbering mess, a first-class weenie, and I don't care about how I look, either. No makeup. No cute outfit. Donned in my old blue sweats, I burrow beneath the warm blanket, a vomit bowl on my chest ready to catch the dry toast I will toss up. All the while, that red poison drips, drips, drips from the bag, through the hose, and into my body.

One more treatment to go.

With my body hair completely gone now, I look like an underfed, sickly adolescent. But, I confess, I love the few benefits of living sans hair. I don't have to shave my legs anymore, which is fabulous, and it takes just seconds to shower and wash my head. Makeup glides on with ease, giving my face a lovely glow that is otherwise absent. And I weigh fifteen pounds less. Yahoo.

Interestingly, my eyebrows and a few eyelashes remain. Go figure. I'm in awe of their sheer pluck and desire to hang on to life. I honor each of them with extra swipes of mascara and several dashes of eyebrow pencil. I love those little guys.

I wear the old sweats to the last treatment and don't bother with makeup. I think I've shrunk. I hate the smell of the place; it smells like chemo cocktail, and so do I. My body reeks of it, sticking to me like gum on a shoe. I'm afraid the stench will stay with me forever.

I finish. It takes over a week for the effects of this last treatment to do its damage, but my spirits are high, soaring. I don't have to go back. Whew.

Two months later, I recline on the exam table. Deft, quick, and efficient, my oncologist's hands move over my breasts, checking the surgical scars. She listens to the even beat of my heart. Smiling, she lays aside her stethoscope.

"You look great, Nikki," she says. "You've successfully completed chemotherapy and radiation and, aside from the tamoxifen, you're done. Now, go live the rest of your life."

The afternoon is quiet, and I'm alone. I'm determined to follow my doctor's advice to go live my life, but I must do one thing first.

Decisive and methodical, I go to my makeup case and toss my red lipsticks into the trash. Next, I grab some large, black garbage bags, move into my closet, and start tossing. In goes anything and everything red: red shoes, red purses, red blouses, red suits, red pants, red lingerie, and red scarves. I scan my closet. Have I missed anything? I look again for the shade of my once-favorite color, the red that will forever remind me of the chemo cocktail. My eyes land on the red, cashmere sweater I wore to the first treatment. I throw it in.

I drag the two full bags outside. Grunting with effort, I kick them to the curb, adrenalin pumping. Defiant, I make the digital gesture. Done.

My son is fine. My husband is taking me to Italy. And I'm on my way to full recovery. Soft hairs have begun to peak from my scalp, my skin glows with health, and my eyes twinkle with vitality.

It's time to make plans . . . for the rest of my life.

—*Nikki Marchesiello*

Warrior Women Wear Pink

I stand there in front of a naked Noble fir, feeling naked clear to my soul.

My mother has just been diagnosed with breast cancer. She is eighty-eight. We are on the brink of Christmas.

Everything that was in me has been hollowed out to make room for pain and anger, and bourbon.

Beside the naked tree is a roll of lovely velvet ribbon. It's pink. What other color is there right now? When you collide with breast cancer, there is no color but pink. And there can be no bows other than the familiar loops that draw us all into some sort of supportive, caring symmetry. You don't tie them; you cut them just right and reverently fold one side over the other, securing each one with a wee dot of adhesive.

This was my tree-decorating mantra—to turn every act of holiday decorating into a war cry. Every beautiful, soft, curved velvet ribbon went onto a spiny tree branch with purpose, as though advancing a battle line.

I remembered Mom wanting to tie pink ribbons in my hair when I was a little girl. I wanted blue; pink was for sissies. Now I am older and wiser. Pink is not for sissies. It's for warrior women.

The blush on my cheeks will not go on gracefully, blended, any longer. It will go on in two distinct lines. I am painted for battle. Because you need a warrior's soul to be strong enough for your mother and for yourself and for the rest of the clan.

You have to shake the tears out of your voice when the grandchildren come for Christmas and ask, "Why is the tree decorated like this?" You explain and bring honor to the unseen collision at hand as Great Grandma sits on the end of the couch with a brave smile. You gently invite babies to give their support to her as she faces her upcoming surgery. And you trust in those young, believing, passionate little faces, as you press pink ribbons off the tree into their hands before they leave, inviting them into the circle of support, because that is where they belong.

Then you turn off the lights and fall face first onto the carpet and cry your eyes out, until your shoulders finally stop shaking and your cat takes pity on you and curls up on your back to bring comfort.

Christmas is coming fast, and the snowflakes in the store windows are taking root inside you and you want to cheer them on so they can freeze your heart into a nice, numb state. But instead your heart escapes the icy snare and snaps back hard the other direction.

You have some extra holiday cheer and then some more, hoping for numbness again. Then, suddenly, you're in tears on the phone, reading the pastor's wife the riot act about the unfairness of something like this happening to someone like Mom, buffeting her with the unanswerable "why?" The tears carry mascara clear down your neck, but the cat still loves you and waits patiently for your sobs to subside enough to make you a suitable place for a nap, and comfort comes in the language of a purr.

Reality builds upon reality, and there are appointments to keep. There is yet another mammogram and installation of something called a "wire" that will come into play during surgery. All I get to know is that it's painful. And all the staff at the breast clinic know it. They honor Mom by bringing blankets warmed in their special oven, and they cocoon her in the best warmth they can give against the cold of technology. The people in the clinic can't take the pain out of the procedure, so they bring another warm blanket to shore her up against it. What else can they do?

The day finally wraps up and gives way to the "time between" as we wait for surgery.

On an especially long night, I decide to send a story tip to Oprah. I tell about Mom rescuing a baby and toddler from a burning home in pre-statehood Alaska and how now, at age eighty-eight, she has breast cancer. I ask if it's possible to find the babies she rescued. But I never hear anything back. I wonder if I should've given the tip to Ellen, instead.

There are still more appointments, and somehow time that once slipped between your fingers is moving like sludge.

You have painfully real talks with your mom about things like lumpectomy versus mastectomy, and somehow the issue of your thighs getting that cottage-cheesy kind of look seems pathetically shallow.

Mom's surgeon has a genuine smile and a sense of humor. I like her.

I take a business card home, and call back later. The receptionist answers. "I'm in charge of your wacky phone call for the day," I announce, and she giggles, so I continue. "I wonder if there's any chance Doctor would consider a special request? Doctor will be doing my mom's breast cancer surgery. And, well, Mom has always wanted pierced ears. Is there a remote chance Doctor would pierce her ears while she is under anesthesia?"

Silence. Followed by laughter. "Well, if any doctor would do it, I expect she would," the receptionist says and promises to check.

The answer comes back no, however.

Mom has always wished her ears were pierced, but the idea of going through the piercing was just too much for her. She said she would have to be sedated to do it. Somehow, this seems like the perfect time. I'm searching hard for anything positive in this murky gray place we're headed toward.

I call the doctor's office again a week later.

The answer is still no.

The next time I see the doctor is just before surgery—with wee diamond studs in my pocket.

"Any chance?" I ask her when she comes to touch base with Mom.

"I don't have the equipment," she says.

I explain that all she needs is a needle. When she says she doesn't know how, we have another short chat. She leaves saying "no promises," but the diamond studs are in her pocket.

Time is supposed to run on a standard measure, although I'm persuaded it moves much slower in surgery waiting rooms. When the doctor comes in to see us, she is all smiles and encouraged about how well things went, about the clear area she was able to get around the tumor.

The gurney carrying Mom isn't far behind her. Looking bleary in her highly attractive surgical cap, my elderly mother reaches up to the side of her face and says, "I have pierced ears!" with a giddy, half-sedated smile.

There is nothing light or humorous about doing battle with the titan of breast cancer. In fact, I am only too happy for this one small respite in the seriousness of the aftermath of recovery.

When Mom's support team of well-wishers calls her to see how things are going, she answers, "Well, it's actually going very well, but my ears are sore."

Her quirky answer is enough to ease the fear for just a moment, and friends from decades ago giggle with her again. The ear-piercing story is like a magical skate key. And for a few minutes, instead of feeling overwhelmed by the hard reality of Mom's cancer, it is as though they have strapped on those hunky old street skates and are holding hands and skating over the obstacles together, as good, long-time friends are supposed to. Now, friends wrap up a phone call they were almost afraid to make with a giggle instead of a tear.

It's just more proof that diamonds can be a girl's best friend. Those little diamond stud earrings are steadfast with my mom. And then we gift the doctor with earrings at every follow-up appointment, and we all laugh together.

One year into Mom's recovery, her deeply treasured, long-lost half sister is diagnosed with breast cancer. A single mom without good insurance coverage, her mammograms had been infrequent, and the diagnosis comes late. Although she is half Mom's age, she passes within a few months, leaving behind a young son.

The burning house Mom had escaped from is still on fire. And far too many other people are not making it safely back into the snowy front yard either.

A day becomes a week, then a month, and a quarter, and seasons give way to each other and we paint with a bolder shade of hope.

As Mom approaches ninety, we plan an epic birthday party. When her surgeon, her oncologist, her nurse practitioner, and her state senator make plans to come, we know we have a rock star on our hands. Her brother flies in from Alaska to surprise her. We also know what a profound gift it is that Mom is doing so well.

Mom's hair is thinning more all the time, a common side effect of tamoxifen, a small toll to pay in the larger scheme of bargaining with matters of life and death.

It is autumn, and the long-lost half-sister that Mom had so little time with has been in her grave for months now. The alarm has been sounded for the family members who never had a chance to meet Ellen, who will only know her as a red flag for medical history sheets, a second close family member with breast cancer.

Now, as she begins her tenth decade of life, Mom is still in the rescue business—but instead of taking dramatic leaps to save babies, she takes baby steps to save herself. Every day that she takes her follow-up medication and cares for her body, it's not so different than it was six decades ago. She knew going in that not everyone comes back out of a burning building. Yet, she was gritty enough to do it and to bring others with her. Maybe she's not carrying babies out this time, but carrying her own burden has been more than enough.

Then again, maybe I'm not looking closely enough. Who am I to say that she walked alone through the smoke-filled burning building of breast cancer? Who may have been setting their own feet into the prints she left behind for them?

Each day dawns, and the pills rattle in the tamoxifen bottle as Mom faithfully follows the protocol. Her cornflower blue eyes don't always give away her secrets, but they can't always hide her private tears. She speaks of "one boob skinnier and longer than the other" and makes light of it, but I know in the quiet of her soul, she remembers her balanced, voluptuous body. Now wisdom and grace have stepped in to take over for that perfect symmetry. And I like to think those two children, now grown, that she carried out of the smoke and fire and darkness so long ago, one in each arm, against each of her then healthy breasts, are somehow wishing Mom well as she continues to battle the blaze raging inside her every single day.

But then, I like to think everyone would. And that if all the people in the world knew Mom's story, there'd be a sudden shortage of pink velvet bows this Christmas.

—*Christy Caballero*

Letter 7

I received the letter on a Thursday evening in midwinter, upon returning home from my Spanish class. It read: "We have found an area in your mammography that we believe is probably benign (not cancer)." This remarkable sentence squirmed under scrutiny. It told me nothing, and it took my breath away.

I was reassured the following morning, when, after a night of little sleep, I went over to the hospital and met with the radiologist, who told me that this was "Letter 7," which is sent to women whose mammograms show scar tissue from previous surgeries. He showed me the slides, pointing out the scar tissue, and seemed genuinely bothered that I'd found Letter 7 to be so alarming. I exited the hospital, reassured but shaken, blinking in the bright sun.

As a cancer survivor, I will always live with the fear of being drawn through the gauntlet of cancer treatment again. I know it can happen, and dread everything about it—the fear of death, the deadpan doctors, the weakness and sickness, losing my hair again. Until that evening, though, that sense of dread had been gradually retreating, settling down. Yet, almost three years after my last radiation treatment, when I'd come to believe with almost certainty that my share of cancer was gone, it took only three words—the terrible first three words of Letter 7, "We have found"—to send me reeling back in time to the moment of my diagnosis.

Right after my biopsy, I sat in a post-surgical recliner, still under the influence of Versed, which makes you not care for a time that the masked man leaning over you is excising part of a potentially malignant tumor. The surgeon appeared, suddenly, like a hologram, now wearing his mask jauntily under his chin, and announced glibly that it was cancer, even though it hadn't yet been examined by a pathologist.

"I can just tell," he said. "I've done hundreds of these." Then he went away.

My husband held my hand. I was still attached to the hospital by an intravenous line. A spooky nurse poked her head through the curtains and told me she would pray for me. She said it twice. I said okay, to keep her from saying it a third time. I was very grateful for another nurse, named Marjorie, who quietly and compassionately helped me get the hell out of there.

I recall a number of days, then, of looking around at my husband and my house and my family and my pets and my friends and trying to wrap my mind around the certainty that I would die and that they would be watching me die and then they would keep on living.

During those awful first days and the weeks and months that followed, the doctors were breezy and nonchalant. They looked off into space as they examined and spoke to me, absently scanning the chrome instruments and gauges that crawled the mauve painted walls. I was given pamphlets covering all aspects of treatment and was soon made to understand that the cancer would be cut and poisoned and burned out of me with fierce dispatch. In those offices with those clinicians, it was as though my fear was unremarkable, beside the point. They'd seen it hundreds, thousands, of times. They breathed it like air.

I had another surgery to remove the rest of the lump and a third to remove lymph nodes. The second anesthesiologist brandished Versed again.

"This is going to make you feel a little bit drunk," he said.

The hospital swung crazily around me as they wheeled me to the operating room.

At the third surgery, a less jolly anesthesiologist proferred Versed. When I refused it outright, she sat at the foot of my bed and pouted.

"You like Versed so much," I snapped, "you take it."

I lost my hair after two weeks of chemo, like everybody does. I was weak and tired during the series of four treatments. The anti-nausea pills worked, and there was no vomiting. I developed an avid disgust for red meat and craved fresh fruit constantly. My white blood cell counts went down as the toxins being pumped into me killed off the fast-growing cells in my body, and back up during the three week breaks between treatments.

Compulsively, relentlessly, I honed my sense of humor. Bald jokes abounded. Once, I made my nephew stop crying by removing my scarf and displaying my stubbly scalp. The doctors were, however, immune to my comedic efforts. Exasperated, at one point, when asked to bare my cancer-free breast for yet another palpation, I told my oncologist, "That's the well-behaved one." I was pleased with this joke and watched her face for a reaction. She grimaced as though experiencing a sudden gas pain.

After chemo, the six and a half weeks of radiation were a piece of cake. I would drive to the cancer center, put on a gown, lie still on the radiation bed for a minute or so, power-walk to the dressing room, get dressed, slam-dunk the gown with a modicum of repressed hostility into the laundry bin, power-walk out of the hospital, and drive back home. I didn't realize how little I was enjoying it until, in the parking lot after my final treatment, I found myself doing a spontaneous little dance of joy. I'd survived. No more hospitals, no more IVs, no more flimsy gowns, and no more mannequinesque doctors witnessing it all with averted eyes. My life expanded around me again.

I now have enough hair to make a ponytail. I have a job I enjoy, I'm writing like crazy, and I'm seeing a lot of movies and reading a lot of books. I've lost any tolerance I might have had for people who are careless of my feelings or who waste my time. I survived, and I'm living my life, but I don't consider having survived a feat of uncommon strength. I don't feel victorious, as the women's magazines urge me to, because to me that implies that I was somehow better at survival than those women who aren't as lucky as I am. Life is different now, I will say that. I am more focused and driven than before. I am more alert, more philosophical. These are good things. But I will never, ever say I'm glad I got cancer. I will never, as I've been urged on occasion, call it a blessing, because it just is not. I am changed and my life is changed. Letter 7 reminded me that my survival does not make me blessed or chosen—just lucky. My fear of cancer returning is still ingrained in me and probably always will be. And I can live with that.

—Karen A. Condon

Probably Nothing

Sometimes, reality strikes with tidal-wave force. This was the year it slammed into me, wave after wave after wave.

I was already grieving for my dad, who was in the latter stages of prostate cancer, when my best friend was fatally injured in an auto crash. She lived eighty days on life support. The night she died, my younger daughter was in surgery at the same hospital for injuries she had incurred in a separate traffic accident. Thankfully, my daughter's injuries were not life-threatening.

Before I could steady my swamped emotions, another wave came rushing at me in the form of a call from my doctor's office. The phone rang at my desk in the news office where I worked as a reporter in Rockford, Illinois. "We spotted something on your mammogram that looks suspicious," said my friendly doctor, JoAnn Holoka.

"We'll schedule a lumpectomy to be sure, okay? Now, you have a nice day," she offered pleasantly.

"A nice day? You've just told me that a cobra might be loose in the room, and I'm supposed to have a nice day?"

She laughed and assured me that it was "probably nothing, but we need to make sure."

Mammogram. The very word sounded like it should be conducted entirely by mail. I fervently wished that were the case and that I could just mail my "suspicious" breast in an envelope.

Later that week, I sat stripped to the waist with my breast squeezed flat by a clamp.

The X-ray technician, a young man, entered the room wearing a lab coat and an irritating grin. "How are you today?" he asked casually.

"Fine," I answered, thinking, *Fine as any woman can be, half naked and clamped by a monstrous device with a needle inserted into her breast while a grinning young man looks on.*

"It's probably nothing," the technician said as he positioned the machine. "But it pays to be sure."

Nothing? The what-ifs kept whispering in my ear. *What if it's not benign? What if it has spread? What if it's too late? What if I die?*

What was I thinking? I chided myself for being morbid and switched my what-ifs to other topics.

What if green hair grows on my chin? What if I'm asked to appear on Dancing with the Stars *and my partner is a Bigfoot creature?* I imagined a few more ridiculous scenarios to remind myself how foolish it is to worry. Despite my moment of forced hilarity, though, the disease remained a very real threat.

That afternoon, the lumpectomy completed, my husband held my hand while the surgeon gave us the news. "I removed the tissue, and . . ." she paused. Her next words washed chillingly over me. ". . . and I don't expect this to be benign. We'll wait for the report from pathology, but I think I should prepare you that we will probably be doing additional surgery, removing the nipple and possibly the entire breast." She spoke calmly, precisely, her clinical voice devoid of emotion.

My husband and I both stared at her, stunned into silence by the reality that what was once "probably nothing" was now probably something serious requiring additional and immediate treatment. Something that could disfigure me. Something that would leave me less than whole. Something that would affect my husband. Something that could even take my life.

The surgeon interpreted my silence. "You're not going to die," she declared, her expression stern.

Somehow, I knew that. The fear of disfiguring scars and a mutilated body seemed more frightening.

I'd once heard a comedian say, "Show me a Jewish girl without great breasts, and I'll show you her uncle who can fix that." I did not have a Jewish uncle who was a plastic surgeon. I did not know what our insurance would cover. In this country, where Hollywood queens regularly augment their bodies, the size of a woman's breasts reveals a lot about our culture. What exactly it reveals, I don't know. I only knew I wanted to keep my body intact.

While we waited on the pathology report, my husband and I went ahead with plans to go on a family vacation. I tried to enjoy the activities, smiling outwardly while inwardly breathing prayers. What would life be like with a flat chest or a lopsided one? Visions of my upper body marred by scabbed-over, gaping wounds tormented my sleep. To make myself even more desperately depressed, I tried on a few bathing suits. "Can I try on a three-piece?" I asked the puzzled clerk "Two for my body and a blindfold for my eyes."

I called my doctor once, long distance, hoping for good news. The Rockford pathologists did not agree on the report, but it "could be nothing," she offered. She added that she had forwarded the tissue slides to the Mayo Clinic for an expert opinion. Nothing definitive yet. I had to continue our travels while wondering if my life would be irrevocably altered when we returned to Rockford.

It was. Mayo Clinic diagnosed an in situ carcinoma. Before I had time to consider my ugly options—a lumpectomy and radiation, or a single or even a bilateral mastectomy and then decide on a method of breast reconstruction—the tsunami of tidal waves struck. I got the news just as I was leaving my conference with a team of health professionals, all urging me to choose radiation. My parents had been in a serious auto accident in Oklahoma that had left them both in the hospital. Dad was not expected to live, and Mom might not recover sufficiently to walk again.

Where was the God I had prayed to and followed as closely as I knew how? Had He abandoned me?

I felt helpless, overwhelmed by a powerful force that was carrying me where I did not want to go. That afternoon, I boarded a plane for Tulsa, Oklahoma, all thoughts of my own health pushed aside. After five days, Dad was moved out of the intensive care unit. Mom had undergone surgery for a broken hip, leg, and wrist. She was going to recover.

Did I dare leave my injured parents to fly back to Illinois and go ahead with the surgery? My doctor insisted. She wasn't certain she had "gotten it all." The disease could be "spreading through" my body, "multiplying at fifty-thousand cells per day."

I decided to get the operation behind me so that I would be sufficiently recovered to be there for my parents when they were released from the hospital. After hugging them one more time, I boarded the plane for Rockford, perhaps the most difficult thing I'd ever done.

Time was of the essence. I said no to radiation, a prolonged course of treatment. My doctors quickly scheduled the mastectomy and the reconstructive procedure.

I was wheeled into the operating room and left alone, the only view from my gurney a ghastly array of enormous devices hanging from the cavernous ceiling. For the first time since my doctor's first unwelcome call, I allowed the tears to flow as I prayed. *Dear God, I'm going to wake up and find myself in a body that will never be the same. I don't know how long my dad is going to live, and my mom is very broken. Where are you?*

At that moment, a nurse walked into the room and spoke to me tenderly. "Oh honey, you're crying. And I won't tell you to stop. You have every right to cry. What they're going to do to you shouldn't happen to any woman. I understand. They're cutting into more than just your body. It's your sense of femininity and your emotions, too."

Having undergone a hysterectomy only two years earlier, I said wryly, "Maybe I'll just start life over as a man. What's left of me will hardly be a woman."

"Now, that's not true. You're a beautiful woman. Is someone here with you? Where's your mother?"

"She's in a hospital in Oklahoma," I sniffed, unleashing a fresh stream of tears.

"Oh, my dear girl! Well, then, you just pretend I'm your mother," she said and wrapped her arms around me. "You have a very good surgeon, and your plastic surgeon also does a good job." Her voice was soothing and her words reassuring, as she rocked me gently, then drew back with a half smile. "He's the same doctor who did my surgery."

"You had this surgery, too?" I asked, glancing at her chest.

"No, honey. I've had a weight problem all my life and finally chose to have my stomach stapled. After I lost the weight, I had an apron of excess skin, and Dr. Weiskopf removed it."

She asked me about my family and said that she had never married. "No man ever wanted me, because I was always so fat."

I felt a stab of compassion for this kindly middle-aged woman, slender and certainly not unattractive. She had missed out on the thrill of romance, the love of a dedicated man, and the comforts of a happy marriage. She had never experienced the sweet delight of cuddling her newborn babe in her arms. Probably, she never would.

My tears stopped in that instant. Why was I feeling sorry for myself? God had given me a wonderful husband and two beautiful daughters. I'd already had several years of a happy family life such as this gentle woman may never know.

I went to sleep and woke up with reconstructed breasts, thinking of my new shape as nothing to be concerned about. I even laughed at what I called my "Dolly Partons" while the overinflated expanders were still in place.

Although the year ahead was filled with complications, a staph infection and follow-up surgeries, the real healing had already taken place. I never knew that nurse's name, but I call her Lilly. From her I learned that when you're walking through a dark and forbidding valley, God sends a lilly of the valley. My lilly of the valley reminded me to count my blessings. And that helped me to hang on to my most trusted life preserver—my faith. The storms of life come to everyone, and the wind and the waves are real, but we can weather and rise above them if we place our trust in God.

—Harriett Ford

Carrying My Head in a Nordstrom's Bag

I t began, as dramas often do, with a telephone call from the doctor: "Yes, it's cancer." (Did he use the "C" word, or did he say "It's malignant"? I can't remember now.) Sitting at the kitchen table, meeting my husband's inquiring gaze as the call ended, I pointed to my left breast and said, "Well, you'd better kiss this sucker goodbye, because it's coming off."

How many times have we heard that our first response is the truest? My humorous remark was purely a reflex action, born of many years of wisecracking. You see, I firmly believe in the old Viennese saying: "It's fatal, but not serious." It's okay to laugh, even in our darkest times.

So began a year of incredible changes—to borrow a phrase from Queen Elizabeth, my medical *annus horribilis*. The particulars might be mildly interesting for those with knowledge of cancer: a diagnosis of stage-three, grade-A invasive ductal carcinoma, seventeen lymph nodes positive for cancer, a modified radical mastectomy, insertion of a subcutaneous venous port, eight rounds of chemotherapy spaced three weeks apart with three different medicines, and six weeks of radiation.

Make no mistake, life during cancer treatments was not fun and games. But I chose humor during those difficult times to make others more comfortable around me. And even now, nearly ten years post-diagnosis, I choose to remember the events lightheartedly.

A few cases in point: To the young hospital technician who expressed concern upon seeing my bruised, biopsied breast, I remarked, "What, this old baseball? It's coming off on Monday." I named the venous port device implanted in my chest "the alien baby," while firmly contending that this "alien" would give me extended life, not suck the life from me. I watched light comedies and romances while receiving chemotherapy. Okay, okay . . . I did watch *Titanic* once, but, hey, we all knew the ship sank.

And I often threatened that, one day, I was going to write a story entitled "Carrying My Head in a Nordstrom's Bag" or "The Year of Living Hairlessly." The part about "carrying my head in a Nordstrom's bag" came from transporting my wig du jour on its Styrofoam form to the gym on exercise days while wearing a turban, color-coordinated to my work-out duds. I would shower and dress for work at the gym, and only once did I forget my head . . . er, my wig!

I vividly remember a pre-dawn trip to the bathroom when I mistook two wigs that were drying in the bathtub as large rodents and went looking for a weapon. Let me tell you, a tennis racket can do terrible things to a wig!

When traveling, did you know that a tall oatmeal container or a flour canister makes a great temporary wig stand? It's true. One night, I was sleeping in a hotel when the fire alarm went off around 2:00 AM. I had noted signs of remodeling in the lobby and figured it might be a false alarm. But I called the front desk to confirm, telling the bemused clerk, "I just want to know if this is serious enough to put on my wig." Luckily, it wasn't.

Being totally hairless had some positive features: No shaving (anywhere). Wigs require washing and styling only once every three weeks. I could be a blonde or a redhead to match my mood or outfit. And every day I had another golden opportunity to create the perfect set of eyebrows using plastic templates and three shades of eyebrow pencils. Thank goodness for cosmetics. If people noticed I had no natural eyelashes or eyebrows, they never mentioned it. And in a wonderfully bizarre show of simpatico, my longest girlfriend inexplicably lost her eyelashes for several months during my treatments.

Sometimes you lose what you love most. I loved my thick hair, my large eyes, and (privately) my chest. Now, I faced a bald head, sunken eyes, and a chest that looked like a train wreck. I had seen my grandmother's chest following her radical mastectomy in 1962; I never knew they made surgical bulldozers, but they used one on her. It was shocking. In my case, the scar is barely noticeable. Did I think of her when I received my cancer news? Yes, I did. But equally devastating were my husband's memories of a nine-year-old boy losing his mother to breast cancer. His mom had died in 1945 at the age of forty-five.

Modern medicine failed to diagnose my cancer early, despite yearly mammograms and special screening tests. But I held fast to the hope that modern medicine could prolong my life . . . if I survived the treatments. Being in good health and relatively young, I opted for the whole a-la-carte menu! I told anyone who asked what chemo was like that I scheduled on my calendar to have the 72-hour flu every three weeks for six months. To keep up my strength, I gave myself permission to eat whatever sounded good whenever I felt like eating it. When was the last time you had three-bean salad and corn on the cob for breakfast? Frankly, it's not that bad. And being a

Hoosier, I can never get enough corn. After all, Indiana is the home state of Orville Redenbacher.

My new "bosom buddy" became my chest prosthesis. The American Cancer Society Reach to Recovery volunteer shared one of her retired forms. I used this loaner for several months before I was emotionally ready to go into a fitting room. When I returned her prosthesis, I included a laminated map of the United States with large colored dots marking all the cities her loaner breast (and I) had traveled to: Washington, D.C., Chicago, Philadelphia, San Antonio, even Hawaii. The map was proof that my life went on. It was extremely bumpy, at times, but as close to normal as we could make it.

Now I have several bosom buddies, sort of like the many-themed Barbie dolls. They are each called "Midge"—a contraction of "My" and "Idge," being as I've lost the "cleave" but still have my "age." There's Sporty Midge for the gym, Sailor Midge for hot tubs and pools, and Best Buddy Midge for regular daily wear. I love them all. Yes, there was that time in the hot tub when I forgot to securely affix Sailor Midge inside my swimsuit and noticed too late that the water-logged breast form had migrated to a stomach pudge. But, hey, *c'est la vie!* Life goes on.

Do I ever get scared about having cancer? Yes, whenever I hear of another person who's been diagnosed. Whenever I visit a friend who has advanced cancer and is gasping for breath. Whenever I get a sharp pain and think, *Is the cancer coming back?* But I consciously choose not to live a fearful life; I strive to live a grateful and joyous life.

When we focus on what we don't have, we feel diminished. The American marketing and advertising industry has done an exceptional job of making us all feel deficient and deprived. Frankly, the economy depends on us wanting more. But when we shift our focus to what we already have, we soon feel a sense of abundance. Some breast cancer friends write daily in their gratitude journals. I don't do that, but not a day goes by that I don't acknowledge my good fortune: My wake-up call wasn't fatal.

I feel most fortunate to have my dear husband beside me every step of the way. An art professor, he reminded me following my mastectomy, "Sweetheart, asymmetry is much more interesting than symmetry." I often told people that I was a "2-4-6 even" person married to a "1-3-5 odd" person. Well, now it appears that I've crossed over to the "odd" side, too.

Attitudes of thankfulness and gratitude have been shown to boost our immune system. When we feel positive, our body's ability to release immune-stimulating endorphins is enhanced. Do I think a positive attitude alone can keep me cancer-free? Definitely not. But I recognize it makes life more enjoyable for me and people around me, and it enables my body to help heal itself.

I'm not discounting or underestimating the role of spirituality during times of crisis and difficulty. I've already hinted at some of these elements in my life: a strong sense of a life force, my belief in a holy spirit that resides in all of us, that feeling of calm that comes when you turn yourself over to the unfolding events with trust and faith in a positive outcome. Am I more religious now than I was ten years ago? No, not really. But I am deeper spiritually than before. And I am more compassionate with people in general—especially the chronically ill.

For what you don't know about me that I'll tell you now is that I was overdue for an attitude adjustment. My compassionate manner toward sick people masked an underlying judgment that somehow they could have avoided their illness if only they had taken better care of their health. I sadly learned that you can do all the "right" things (exercise, eat a healthy diet, not smoke, get regular checkups, do self-exams) and *still* get the shock of your life. Once you experience that, you can despair and stay bitter, or you can GET OVER IT and get better. In my mind, if you stay bitter, you won't get better. What I can't stress enough is this: trust your instincts. If you think something is amiss in your body, don't be dissuaded from further testing. Your insistence could save your life.

People sometimes tell me, "You are so brave, so courageous." Believe me, I'm not. To me, the face of courage is a firefighter who enters a burning building on the verge of collapse or a police officer who comes between a bullet and an innocent bystander. I wanted to be a survivor and was determined to do whatever it took to stay alive. Most of you would make the same decision.

In my wallet, I carry a card with the six traits of a survivor. Number one on the list is "A sense of self-esteem." Number two is "A sense of humor," and number four is the "Ability to bear discomfort without losing hope." My lifelong tendency to reframe negative events with a touch of wit enabled me to navigate the rough times with confidence in a positive outcome.

"We've been given a gift," a mother told me after tragically losing her teenage son in a car accident. "And it's called the present."

Author Sarah Ban Breathnach put it this way: "Learning to live in the present moment is part of the path of joy."

So, ultimately, the secrets of my survivorship are simple: keep laughing and keep breathing. The secret of my success is . . . I'm living!

—*Jennifer S. Kutzik*

In the Eye of the Sparrow

Inflammatory breast cancer. "It's rare as hen's teeth," my obstetrician assures me as he examines my swollen breast during my routine prenatal appointment. "You don't have it." He explains that IBC is the rarest and most aggressive form of breast cancer, accounting for only 2 to 5 percent of breast cancers but particularly deadly.

My left breast aches in his hands. For two months, it has been significantly larger than the right. Hard, streaked with red, and hot to the touch, it bulges from the sides of my bra. The doctor thinks that, rather than IBC, I have an abscess caused by untreated mastitis, an infection of the mammary gland, which sometimes affects pregnant women.

"When you hear hoof prints in the night," he says, "assume it's horses, not zebras."

Nevertheless, a biopsy shows that I do, indeed, have cancer.

I meet for the first time with my oncologist, Dr. Cheryl Jones. The waiting room is full of men and women, most of them elderly. At thirty-five and pregnant, I don't recognize myself among these cancer patients. But Dr. Jones, who is young and wears high heels under her lab coat, immediately puts me at ease. She assures me that, because I am in the fifth month of pregnancy, chemotherapy will not harm my unborn son. I relax, knowing I've found someone I can trust.

I've noticed that people who aren't facing a life-threatening disease—the people I work with every day—are not happier than I am. They let themselves get angry and miserable about things that don't matter or that matter fairly little. Before I got ill, I couldn't sleep at night because I was so stressed out about what kind of house to buy. Now, I no longer feel the need for a big house. I've let that "need" go.

The turning point came a couple of days after the diagnosis, when I realized that I would not trade my life, with cancer, for anybody else's life. Of course, I'd much rather not be ill. That's my goal. But if this is the life I've been given, then I have to accept it as mine. I wouldn't want to be anyone else.

Most people haven't seen a chemotherapy room.

The nurse leads me into a sunny lounge full of reclining chairs. In each chair, a patient sits reading, watching TV, or dozing while IVs drip. I settle down with my novel.

The middle-aged woman perched on her husband's chair next to me turns and introduces herself. "This is my husband. They call him Rattlesnake. I'm Mrs. Rattlesnake."

What does this place remind me of? These men and women talking, joking, sleeping, eating. Laughter that sometimes verges on hysterical. Gossip about soap operas, the clapping and whooping of Oprah's audience on the television set. Then I remember: a high school cafeteria.

Anger. At the supermarket I see an obese woman buying a carton of cigarettes. She must be seventy years old. Alive. *How unfair*, I think, *that I've taken such good care of my health all my life, and yet I'm the one suffering with cancer.*

In the baby shop, the pregnant woman in front of me complains that she already has two boys. She sits her five-year-old son on the counter and says, pointing to her belly, "If this one is a boy, I'll love him anyway. But I really want a girl."

You ungrateful woman, I want to scream. *Here I am, fighting to live, fighting to give birth to my son, and you whine about three healthy children.*

I am unhappy that my hair is falling out. I am developing a bald patch on either side of my forehead, as though I have a receding hairline. Where the hair falls out, my skin is very pale and has wispy fuzz on it, like a baby's. After I finish shampooing, my hands are covered with wet hair. I wash it only every other day now and try not to comb it, because the comb pulls out a lot of hair, too.

The main thing I fear is not looking and feeling normal. I don't like feeling like there is an invisible wall between me and healthy people.

I find comfort in prayer. A friend of my mother's has sent me a prayer shawl, and every morning I drape it over my head and pray, thanking God for life and praying for healing. Whenever I pray, Noah, perhaps sensing the feeling of well-being pervading me, begins to turn and kick inside of me. We stand together, talking to God.

I've refused to bring an overnight bag to the hospital. Two days earlier, the doctors sent me home from the same delivery room because I was not well enough to give birth. My husband, Andy, held me in the parking lot as I wailed.

But today the nurse smiles as she reads the lab report. My white blood cells have rebounded. "We're all set," she says. "We can start the drip."

I adjust the cap on my bald head. I have already endured twelve weeks of chemotherapy. Now, it's time to give birth to my son.

The petocin kicks in quickly, and my contractions intensify. In just three hours, I am fully dilated and ready to push. With Andy standing at my head and a nurse between my legs, I push for a grueling two hours. Then, suddenly, I feel my son slide out of my body and hear the loud wail as he feels the cold air on his body.

At almost six pounds, Noah is born healthy and normal. By the time he is checked, cleaned, and swaddled, he has fallen asleep. I hold him in my arms and think, overwhelmed with relief, *He is worth losing a breast for.*

A month after Noah's birth, I'm back on chemo. This time, I'm getting a Taxotere treatment every three weeks and weekly infusions of the new wonder drug, Herceptin. I've been warned that Taxotere is often difficult to tolerate, and indeed, I soon take to calling it "taxo-terror." Two days after each treatment, I am hit with exhaustion unlike any I have felt before. I am wrung out, unable even to climb out of bed. When Noah cries, I bring him into bed with me, coaxing him with a bottle and trying to relax him into sleep. I try to concentrate on his first smiles, on his newly fat face.

Being needed by Noah keeps me from embracing victimhood. No matter how tired I am, no matter how anxious or angry, I have to heat his milk every three hours, change his diaper, and hold him when he cries. I'm not only monitoring the changes in my breast—the increasing softness that indicates the shrinking of my tumor—I'm also noticing the almost daily changes in Noah: the first tentative smiles, the way he wrinkles his forehead and purses his mouth when I pick him up, how intently he looks me in the face. I am grateful for the joy he brings me even in the midst of fear, for the grace of each moment.

As my hair starts to grow, covering my head with the faintest fuzz, Noah loses his first pale fringes. When I hold him to me, our bald heads touch.

One morning, Andy, Noah, and I go out for breakfast. Of course, all the waitresses ooh and ahh over Noah, alert in his car seat. When the middle-aged couple sitting behind us gets up to leave, they stop by our table.

She says, "We've been watching you, and we've decided you're in love."

It's good to be reminded of the continued happiness in my life, despite the struggle.

Four weeks after my last chemotherapy treatment, Andy and I go to the Winship Cancer Center of Emory University for my surgery. Shortly after anesthesia is administered, I tell the nurse, "I feel like I'm getting a little woozy."

She nods and smiles.

When I wake up three hours later, I'm in recovery. Looking down at my bandaged chest, I feel relief rather than trauma. Although I've always liked my breasts, after having cancer, I can no longer view them merely as decorative and pleasurable; now they are a potential threat to my life, as well.

I finally unwrap the gauze and look at my scar. It's long, maybe four to five inches, and purplish, but on the whole, not too scary. It's strange to look at my chest and see one breast gone and to have a flatness where I'm used to seeing a shape, but on the whole, the absence of a breast is not that bad.

It's funny: I'm bald, and I have no eyebrows and no left breast. Yet, I don't feel more insecure about my appearance. On the contrary, looking pretty is far less important to me than it used to be. To tell the truth, it's a freeing experience not to care about my appearance for the first time in my life. I've always known, intellectually, that looking "good" is socially determined, but I didn't know it in my bones until I got cancer. Take my relationship with my breasts, for instance: I used to love my breasts and want to show them off. Now, who cares? They're fat and skin. Cancer strips away the superfluities.

For six weeks, five days a week, I go to the hospital for radiation. I become accustomed to lying on the table while the technicians adjust me. I allow myself to be just a body, to let women's hands move and turn me. It's surprisingly comforting to allow this touch, to be taken care of.

When the technicians leave the room and the ultraviolet light from the machine buzzes above my skin, I imagine white light entering my body, destroying any rogue cancer cells left in the skin. I close my eyes and pray.

I begin attending yoga classes. One of the only places where I feel truly relaxed and at peace is on my yoga mat, sinking my knees and stretching my arms into the pose of a warrior, closing my eyes and focusing on nothing but breath. At these times, I don't worry about cancer. I'm focused only on the movements, on the way my belly expands to take in air.

Before cancer, I felt invulnerable. Cancer was something that happened to other people: old people, smokers, overweight people. But instead, it happened to me. I have always valued control and stability. To cede control, to realize that the forces of life and death are beyond ultimate human power, is a realization that I find liberating. It diminishes me, and yet at the same time, it comforts me to put myself into perspective as part of natural and divine forces that affect every living creature and that I am powerless to stop.

One morning, watching a sparrow, it occurs to me that this bird has mastered the practice of mind that I aspire to in my yoga practice and in prayer: an ability to live as much as possible within the moment, to focus completely on a particular action for its own sake, and then to complete that action and move to another. To exist without anxiety and anger. Sitting at my window watching the sparrow, I think, *It is enough.* It is enough to sit here now, alive and healthy, listening to the cicadas whirring unseen in the branches and to the spatter of my fountain. It is enough to lie in bed with my husband and son, watching the morning sunlight coming through the blinds. It is enough to be here now, fully, without wondering how many of these days I have before me, without asking questions that can bring fear.

It is enough.

—*Anya Silver*

Survival of the Fittest

Fourteen years ago, at the age of forty-seven, I was diagnosed with breast cancer. I'm revered for my organizational skills, but "Do cancer" was something I never scheduled in my Day Planner.

It began so innocently. I was talking on the phone with my sister-in-law when I felt a substantial lump under the armpit by my left breast. *No!* my inner voice screamed. *No, you did not feel anything. It's just the way you're standing or sitting or breathing.* The *Kama Sutra* doesn't include as many positions as I did trying to disprove what my instincts told me were so, even while my mind tried to dissuade me otherwise. Not being one to ignore any impending or imagined disaster, I quickly hung up the phone—"Gotta go, gotta go"—and called the breast surgeon's office. Over the nurse's objection—"I'm afraid he can't fit you in today"—I replied, "I'll be in his office in less than an hour. Make room!"

On my way to the doctor's office, I daydreamed about all the things he would say to reassure me: *Oh, it's nothing. It's just a cyst, just a gland, just a . . .*

"It's moving, and it's soft; that's a good sign," the doctor said as he examined me.

Safe! I could hear the umpire yell.

I had just relaxed my clenched jaw when, upon examining the other breast, he asked, "What's this? Have you ever felt this before?"

When I was a child, my mother often said, "You can only dance at one wedding at a time." I was still dancing to the mass on my left side. What was this now on the right?

"Do you feel that?" the doctor asked, taking my hand and pressing it firmly on my right breast.

"No," I whispered. All I could feel was my heart pounding.

"We'll biopsy this now," his gentle voice blasted in my ears.

"What about the lump on the left side?" I murmured.

"That one has to be surgically removed in order to biopsy it," he answered apologetically.

The powder-blue examining room was turning murky gray. I felt my throat tighten.

"You'll feel a little sting," he said, as he took a needle aspiration of the right breast. "I'll call you with the results on this. Next Friday, we'll remove the mass on the left as an outpatient procedure."

Four long days later, the results of the aspiration came back: benign. With that information and the doctor's encouraging words about the other side— "It's moving, and it's soft"—I headed for the lingerie section at Bloomingdale's department store to reward my breasts.

"Would you please show me the most elaborately decorated and ridiculously expensive bra you have?" I gushed at the saleswoman.

Her face lit up with delight. "Wacoal, definitely Wacoal," she whispered, as though it was sequestered behind the counter, reserved only for the Mercedes of breasts.

"Perfect," I replied. "Please bring me one—no, two—of them."

The doctor called the next day. "The cells in your right breast were benign but slightly irregular. I'd like to remove that entire section and re-biopsy it when we do the other procedure on Friday."

My fifth grade teacher, Miss Mesmer, came to mind, with her ruddy complexion and heaving body, pursing her lips and shaking her finger, "Better safe than sorry."

Friday, the surgery went as planned and that night the preliminary results came back: malignant . . . both breasts. My husband and I embraced many times that weekend, but we barely spoke, fearing that to say "cancer" out loud would make it true. We were to meet with the doctor on Tuesday to discuss my options.

In the doctor's office, I thought of all the women who had sat in the same brown leather chair, nails digging into the tufted arms, dealing with the same sobering news. *How should I conduct myself?* I wondered. I remembered seeing a T-shirt that read, "Cancer is not going to get this bitch." *I could be that,* I coached myself. *I could do this.* I squared my shoulders and lifted my quivering chin.

The doctor smiled slightly and said, "There's been a change in the pathology."

"Fabulous!" I turned to my husband. "They read someone else's chart. Let's go."

No such luck.

The doctor continued, "The tumor on the right breast is malignant, but the tumor on the left is actually a fatty tumor, a lipoma, and it's benign. They look similar on preliminary black-and-white slides, but the color slides showed the distinctions between the benign and malignant cells."

My mind wandered to a segment in the movie *Chinatown,* when Jack Nicholson kept slapping Faye Dunaway's face, back and forth, as she tried to explain her incestuous relationship with her father.

"He's my father, my husband, my father, my husband." Camera. Action. "It's malignant, it's benign, it's malignant, it's benign."

Still-cancer-but-less-of-it seemed a strange thing to celebrate, but my husband and I did. We felt empowered.

I'm superstitious and a person of convenient faith. I don't step on cracks; I only pick up pennies that are heads up; and I see "signs" in everything, from a rainbow to a missed train. This time, I clearly felt as though I had God's hand on me. Six months earlier, I had a normal mammogram. The lipoma propelled me into the doctor's office, enabling him to find cancer on the other breast, which had felt perfectly normal to me. What were the odds?

After a number of opinions, I decided on a mastectomy, chemotherapy, and reconstruction of the right breast and reduction of the left breast. It was the choice I felt I could live with in the years to come when I would be awake, ruminating, at three o'clock in the morning.

I knew what I had to do and remained as focused as I could. I've always had a sense of the absurd, and as serious as cancer is, there were many occasions during the process when I could have used a sidekick to laugh with at the insanity of some of the situations.

My breast surgeon highly recommended a plastic surgeon for the reconstruction, and I made an appointment with him. My first impression was that he was cocky and very short, even with the elevated heels on his cowboy boots. Obviously, an overachiever with a strong ego.

"So, how large would you like the breast?" he asked, as he measured the area for a saline implant.

"How large? I have cancer. I just want it out, and then you can give me what you can."

He looked at me, relieved. "That's good to know, because some women, wanting bigger breasts, give me a difficult time."

No wonder, since his next question was, "In which direction would you like your nipple to lean—east, west, north, or south?"

What was I, a compass? "In which direction?" I gasped. "You've got to be kidding me."

"Oh, no," he replied. "I consider myself an artist and have worked many years to develop my artistic skills."

"Just so you know," I blurted out. "Personally, I'm more interested in your math skills."

I couldn't help thinking, *What the hell am I doing here?* But then I quickly reconsidered. Why choose a surgeon who had no confidence? This guy was for me. I later learned I'd made an excellent choice.

The day of the surgery, the plastic surgeon marked my breast with magic markers, as guidelines for the breast surgeon. As he diligently drew circles, squares, and triangles on what was soon to be my vacant right chest, he looked up and asked, "What pain meds are they giving you for the mastectomy?"

"Forget that. What pain meds are you giving me for the magic markers?" I said, my dignity severely challenged.

In the operating room the anesthesiologist smacked his head into the light fixture—*whack!*— right before he was to inject me. "Are you okay?" he asked, his voice shaking.

"More important, are you okay?" I asked.

The titter of laughter assured me he was, and when I woke up in the hospital room, my "Gumbies," my husband and my sister, were there. These fiercely loving and loyal people would twist and turn for me and be whatever I needed them to be during the long haul of treatment and beyond. My husband fulfilled his "for better or worse" vow a thousand times over.

My oncologist, a man I greatly respect, recommended chemotherapy, so I took his advice. My first session was in a room with many other people. We stole glances at each other and smiled apologetically as though we all had found ourselves at a singles bar.

"This is my first time," I heard myself say as though my virginity were in question.

Six months of chemotherapy made me slightly nauseous (something like my old Monday morning sensations after a pig-out on a Sunday night).

My cancer should have been as afraid of me as I was of it. The cavalry came: My family and friends circled the wagons. My doctors were tenacious and caring. And my confidence in healing was unwavering. These proved to be strong ammunition against an insidious enemy. I had endured and survived.

At the end of all the treatments—the biopsies, the surgeries, the tamoxifin, the breast expander, and the six months of chemotherapy—my breast surgeon asked me, "So, who is the hero?" Even though he was a major force in saving my life, I took a deep breath, looked him directly in his piercing blue eyes, stuck out my renovated breasts, and replied, "Me!"

—*Linda Holland Rathkopf*

Lessons from the Chemo Room

My husband hated the chemo room from the moment we entered the oddly shaped room at the back of my oncologist's office. Seven La-Z-Boy recliners were set around the room, accompanied by side tables for drinks, magazines, and chairs for guests. A nice enough setup, right? So what was the problem?

You'd think it might be the poison or the cancer that scared my husband off. Not so. It was the atmosphere of the place that kept him wishing he were somewhere else. Where was the Zen fountain, the dim lighting, he wondered. What would be wrong with a little piped-in music or hushed silence, even, to bring on a meditative mood?

For my part, I suppose my expectations were much in line with my husband's. For that first appointment I had packed a bag filled with things I thought I'd need during the nearly three hours I'd be receiving my intravenous cocktail. I had a few bottles of water, a granola bar, hard candy, multiple magazines, a book, and my Treo so I could answer e-mail. I was prepared for a long, quiet, sullen time.

The truth is, during the six months I went to chemotherapy, I never read a single magazine. I never cracked a book. There was much too much going on in the chemo room.

The chemo room at my oncologist's office was not a quiet place, and it certainly wasn't sullen. It was a chatty place. Full of laughter and noise, this was a space where people came together and shared their stories. We talked about our kids and provided one another with makeup tips and wig-shopping advice. It was full of mothers and sisters and friends, grand-mothers, spouses, and singles. It was loud and bois-terous, full of life, and, well...the complete antithesis of what my husband and I had expected.

In the end, for me, chemotherapy was about more than the drugs, the La-Z-Boy, or the experience of sitting there receiving my treatment. It was about the people I met and the lessons I learned. Here are just a few.

There Are Many Definitions of Survivor
Hannah was the elder stateswoman in the chemo room. During an impromptu conversation about hair regrowth one day, she informed us in her heavy

eastern European accent, "My hair grew back curly the first time, straight the second, and—" running a hand through her thick hair, "gray the third!"

Three times this woman had sat through chemo. I crossed my fingers that I would be there only once.

As the conversation continued, Hannah informed those of us listening that, in addition to being in the chemo room three times, she was a Holocaust survivor from Czechoslovakia. She had endured Auschwitz, Treblinka, and Bergan–Belson. Hannah's positive attitude in the face of, well, her whole life, served as an inspiration every time I went to chemotherapy.

In my heart, I still only want to be in the chemo room once, but as I look forward to someday reaching the five-year cancer-free mark, I remind myself that there are many definitions of "survivor."

There Might Be an Angel in the Next La-Z-Boy Over

My second time at chemo, my port wasn't working. I'd had the small disk installed near my collarbone, so the nurses could plug in my IV without potentially causing damage to the veins in my arms. But that day it wasn't working. I raised my hands. I touched my toes. I looked left. I shimmied my shoulders. I did everything the nurses could think of, but still the medicine wasn't flowing.

A tall, blonde woman named Melissa was sitting in the chemo lounger across from me. When I'd first walked in that day, we'd shared pictures of our kids. Hers were preschool-aged girls, blonde and angelic. Mine were slightly older, elementary-aged, two boys and a girl. Melissa and I had bonded over photos and parenting stories. When she saw that my drip wasn't flowing, she rolled her own IV pole over near mine. She dropped to the floor and, without asking, rolled up my jean's leg. She began to rub her thumb along my shin, stroking a crevasse between the muscle and the bone. I looked up. The IV was flowing!

When she'd drop her hand, the IV would stop. Before returning to her own La-Z-Boy, Melissa taught my friend, who'd come with me that day, how to rub my leg to get the IV flowing again. When asked how she knew this mysterious way to make my port flow, she told me that she had stage IV cancer. She had been given only months to live and had outlived everyone's expectations. During the time she'd been in chemo, she'd learned a few tricks.

I was grateful. Just before Melissa left the room, I asked her what she'd done for a living before she had been diagnosed. She said she was a harpist. Her daughters may have looked angelic, I realized, but Melissa was the real deal.

Be Aware That Not All the
People You Meet Will Be Positive

Inspiration comes in many forms in the chemo room, if you simply take the time to talk to people. But there are also people who exude negative energy, and before you talk to that person sitting next to you, it is impossible to know which side they will fall on. It is up to you to decide if meeting people in the chemo room is worth the risk. If not, iPods and DVD players can be a girl's best friend.

One day I met a woman who claimed that her cancer was exactly like mine. Stage one, node-negative, same identifying markers. Same chemo. *Just like me,* I thought. Then her story became one of recurrence, higher staging, negative prognosis. This wasn't her first time in the chemo room, it turned out; it was her third. She'd been to Mexico for alternative treatment and had gotten an infection. And the liturgy went on. It was too much for me. I quickly excused myself and went to the bathroom, but the damage was done. Weeks later, I still thought of her story. And I was scared that her story would become mine.

I know now that her story wasn't, and isn't, my story—but sometimes a story like that gets stuck in your head and you can't get rid of it.

That was not the first nor the only time I wished I'd brought a movie to watch. But it's the chance you take if you decide to take the risk of talking to people in chemo. For me, the risk was worthwhile, because I met Melissa and Hannah and many other incredible people whose stories propelled me up and forward.

Chemo Can Provide Its Own Comedy

There are moments in life my friends call, "Stacia moments." I tend to be a bit forgetful, even before chemo, and a whole lot clumsy. My first day in chemo, as I rushed to the bathroom, I forgot to ask the nurse to lower my IV pole. I managed to ram the doorframe, knocking a clock off the wall and breaking it. I still wonder if my HMO will pay for that one.

During my second chemo visit, I stood up too fast and nearly fell off my very cute new platform sandals. The moral here involves wearing flat shoes. If you don't believe me, go ahead, wear high heels to chemo. Don't say I didn't warn you.

On a recent visit the nurse taped to the IV pole a syringe of medication to raise my blood counts that they give me after my chemo, so it would be room temperature by the time I received it. This was not the first time she'd taped the shot to the pole, but this time, another bathroom trip sealed my fate. On my way back, I grabbed the pole right where the shot was (don't ask how I managed that one), knocking off the lid and stabbing myself with the needle. It didn't really hurt or even bleed, but it quickly became the "Stacia" chemo story my family loves to retell.

Chemo sucks. But it can also be the place where you will meet people with invaluable wisdom to share, where you will laugh a little, where you will learn a lot, and where—if you are lucky—you will find the inspiration you need to focus on kicking your cancer out and letting life in.

I am glad the chemo room wasn't a meditative place with a nice fountain and soft elevator music. There is too much I would have missed if I had closed my eyes and drifted away.

—*Stacia Deutsch*

This story was first published in Women and Cancer Magazine, *winter 2006.*

Dear Tumor

Dear Tumor,

I guess this letter is somewhat overdue. You showed up at my house a little more than two years ago, and I have yet to share my thoughts with you. I did not know you before you barged into my life. In fact, you were the farthest thought from my mind. I ran ten marathons before we met. I ate relatively healthy (except for my cookie vice). I was not overweight. I only drank alcohol socially. I had three children and breastfed them all. I was a single parent and an emergency room charge nurse. I did not have time for you, your visit, or your baggage! I was lucky to find time to get my mammogram.

But, despite my protest, you came anyway. I received the news while I was getting highlights at my hair salon. Trust me, I was not getting dressed up for you. My surgeon called my cell to tell me you had arrived. That's when I learned your name: invasive lobular carcinoma. In shock and disbelief, I left the salon and headed home. I was scared. I needed to tell someone. So I did what anyone would do who needed comfort: I called my mom. She had one of your relatives, ductal carcinoma in situ, visit her five years earlier. When I told her you had come for a visit, she told me I needed to fight. She said thousands of women have seen you before and beat you. She assured me I would, too. The problem was, I wasn't a fighter. Given the option of fight or flight, I'd always chosen to fly. Now, what was I going to do?

I was tired. I had battled rheumatic fever, two miscarriages, a bad marriage, a nasty divorce, and raised three kids by myself. My resources were exhausted. I had no idea how I was going to handle things. I hated you and everything you stood for.

When they said you were invasive, they were not kidding. You infiltrated my whole life. I was deathly afraid of you and your potential. You had the power to destroy. My active imagination had you demolishing everything around me. I was sure you would ruin every relationship I knew. How were my kids going to deal with this? They still needed me. What about my boyfriend? Would he still find me desirable? What about my friends? How could I be a good friend if I was broken? What about my bills? My running? My breasts? My hair? My job? My life? Suddenly, everything I knew became fragile. I cried myself to sleep more nights than not. For such a small tumor, I became hugely obsessed with you. You left your mark on everything I did. Your intrusion was overwhelming. I was afraid, and I could not escape.

Even after you were cut out and taken to the lab, I could feel your presence in everything I did. Like a bad houseguest, you left my life a mess. The cleanup was horrendous. Chemo, reconstructive surgery, tamoxifen, treatment for a blood clot, treatment for an ulcer, and gallbladder surgery were just the beginning. Your fingerprints were everywhere. The more I realized this, the more I tried to erase you. I read books. I Googled you. I dwelled on you. I even went to counseling to try to forget about you. I just wanted my life put back together.

But no matter how hard I tried, my back-together life didn't look the same as the life I knew before you. Somewhere along the way, things changed. With all my frustration, I'd somehow missed the gifts you brought. I was so wrapped up in the agony you delivered that I missed the blessings right before my eyes. They surrounded me. These were not the gifts you find on Christmas morning or on your birthday. These were much different; they had value that couldn't be measured. They were treasures. As I uncovered them, one by one, I became less resentful of your intrusion. I realized I had been blessed by your bittersweet appearance.

Some blessings are obvious. We know they are there, but it isn't until we are forced to look deeper that we realize how truly precious they are. My kids all surprised me in one way or another during this journey. My oldest, Krissie, has always been a free spirit. Her happy-go-lucky personality and charisma ooze from her pores. During my treatment, Krissie called frequently to check in and often stopped by. She gave me advice, quoted Dr. Phil, and managed to make me laugh when life didn't seem so funny. Krissie and her animated charm offered me mini-vacations from you, my unwelcome guest, Breast Cancer.

In contrast, my middle child, Nick, was more introspective and quiet. Out of my three children, his personality is most like mine. Because of this, we can go long periods with speaking very little to each other and still be on the same page. When he does speak, our thoughts are one. This was particularly true after my mastectomy. Sitting next to me in his pink bandana, worn for support, he told me he was angry. He said everyone was saying it was going to be okay. He did not feel it was okay. He had spoken my thoughts out loud. It was not okay! What is okay, anyway? If they take two breasts and an arm, is that okay? How about two breasts, an arm, and a leg? His ability to understand and our intuitive connection are gifts I will have forever.

My youngest son, Tim, has always been more vocal. Like his dad, he has never been one to struggle with words. This gift he possesses became more pronounced during my treatment. He was the only one of my kids living with me at the time, and not a day went by that he did not ask how I was feeling. He wore a pink bandana under his lacrosse helmet. He put a pink ribbon on his car. He wore a pink shirt for his high school graduation pictures. I felt his support on every level. On my last day of chemo, Tim presented me with a pink cake that said "Congratulations." He also had shaved his head "so we could grow out our hair together." I cried. Then he topped this act on Mother's Day, when he wrote and read a sermon for the church about our journey through cancer. He brought the place to tears with his heartfelt emotion and honesty. I have never been more proud nor felt so loved.

My boyfriend, Eric, showed his love in more practical ways. Since he was the one who detected you early, he is responsible for my promising prognosis. I shudder to think of the outcome had he not been so perceptive. He was there for every treatment and distracted me with his never-ending thoughts of golf. He let me be my own guide and did not let me wallow in self-pity. He supported my decisions and offered advice when he felt it was necessary. When I was debating on whether to get a bilateral mastectomy or just a right-sided mastectomy, he gave me advice I will never forget. He told me when you change the tires on a car, you change them both at the same time, even if only the right side needs it. So my mastectomy soon became referred to as a tire change. And my perspective changed.

My friends became more important than ever during this challenging journey. Whereas Eric was practical, they offered compassion and empathy. My running friends, Chris and Susan, ran slowly so I could keep up with them. My best friend, Karen, listened to me cry and laugh, and supported every emotion in between. She planned, and paid for, a trip to Mexico to celebrate my recovery. Two of my dearest friends, Sarah and Elizabeth, called frequently to let me know they were there.

Elisa, my friend and coworker, coordinated a plan where all my coworkers prepared meals for me and my family during my treatment. She also organized a fundraising benefit that raised thousands of dollars to help pay for my medical bills. My coworkers no longer felt like acquaintances; they became an integral part of my support system. They wore pink bracelets to show their support. They bought me a gift certificate to a local spa. They tolerated my chemo brain and helped me adjust my schedule around treatments. The paramedics that bring patients to the emergency room, where I worked, asked about me daily. They even gave me a calendar, filled with pictures of local firefighters, and had it signed. I'd never doubted that I worked with the greatest people in the world, but going through this experience truly reinforced it.

It did not take me long to realize that you chose to visit me for a reason. Although I can't explain it, I know that my search for understanding has led me to seek more spiritual guidance. I have always believed in God, but my knowledge of Him was limited. After your visit, I found myself needing more. That is when my son Nick introduced me to church and to the teachings of Pastor Jim. From day one, I felt a connection and a sense of belonging. I believe this was divine intervention. Jim's humor and warmth sparked an interest in me that has only grown in time. His teaching has helped me to understand and accept the changes that I have endured. He has helped me in ways he will never know. I will be forever grateful for the way the church has enhanced my life.

My belief in divine intervention was further validated in the middle of my treatment when I received a call from Katy. Katy is an amazing photographer who put together a book of photographs of breast cancer survivors. At that time, she was looking for someone in the middle of treatment to photograph. I was tired, bald, pale, dealing with a blood clot in my arm, nauseous, and feeling as ugly as anyone could feel. I had three treatments down and three to go. I had no idea what to expect, but I felt if these photographs could alleviate the fear for someone else, my time and effort would all be worth it. The photographs turned out incredible! Katy was able to find, and capture on film, every emotion I felt. Later, she took pictures of my boys and me with our bald heads and again captured emotions I will forever treasure.

The gift that is the least tangible, but probably the most life-changing, is my outlook on life. Until I was faced with my own mortality, I didn't really appreciate things like I do now. I probably have more questions now than answers, but I do view things in a new light. My family, my friends, my church, and all the relationships I was so afraid of losing have only grown stronger. I treasure things I didn't treasure before, and I stopped putting value on other things. I know this is different for everyone, but my life will be forever altered from the visit of one little tumor like yourself.

So, Tumor, in closure, I want to thank you for all you did for me. You helped me to be a better person. I will continue to run the Race for the Cure, to snowshoe in the Romp to Stomp Out Breast Cancer, to walk in the two-day Avon Walk for Breast Cancer, to play golf in Rally for the Cure, to eat at the annual Power of the Promise luncheon, to participate in Relay for Life, and to do whatever else it takes to keep you away from my friends and family. But you definitely changed my life, and for that I will count my blessings. Thank you.

Gratefully,
Julie

P.S. Please don't come back!

—*Julie A. Whitney*

Filling Up and Spilling Over

The first thing my best friend did after her diagnosis was throw herself a party.

My friend, Cissy Taylor, had just one request: that each guest bring her a hat or scarf in anticipation of her chemo-induced baldness. So we did—offering regal turbans, exotically patterned scarves, cozy knit caps, broad-brimmed panamas, and flowered hats.

The hat party was attended by roughly thirty women—among them cops' wives who had befriended her during the ten years she was a police reporter for the local daily newspaper, journalist friends, neighbors, her physical therapist, the county attorney, daughters of friends, and camping buddies. Some were breast cancer survivors, the rest friends who were now more sharply aware that any day one of us could join her unwelcome sorority.

We talked, laughed, and ate. Cissy would never have a party without lots of good food. She tried on all her gifts, considering each with an expression of combined merriment and gratitude. She presented each of us with a wine glass adorned with pink flowers on it, as a thank-you gift and to remind us to do monthly self-exams and to get annual mammograms.

Then came another, unexpected gift. When the gaiety had died down, one of the guests, Liz Anker, a professional singer, broke into a spontaneous song, her liquid contralto introducing us to the lyrics of the Cris Williamson song, "Waterfall."

"Sometimes it takes a rainy day / Just to let you know everything's gonna be all right," Liz began, her voice now the only sound in the room. The rest of us sat or stood, frozen in time, as she continued singing.

Soon, we were all joining in on the refrain, which we sang over and over, in voices choked and jubilant. "Filling up and spilling over, it's an endless waterfall . . ."

Spill, we did—both tears and laughter—as we all surveyed the room, locking eyes with women, some of whom had been strangers just an hour earlier, and sharing what we all knew was a magical moment.

As many of us realized later, that magical moment of sisterhood was Cissy's gift to us. Unorchestrated but unsurprising, coming, as it did, from Cissy, it was one of many gifts she would give us during the course of her treatment and recovery. For those who were facing cancer as well for those of us who someday might, she was showing us how to do it.

Surround yourself with people who care about you, was her message. Anticipate your needs. Don't be afraid to ask for help. Keep music and love in your life. Show your gratitude, even when you're hurting. Perhaps most important, keep your sense of humor.

Cissy, then fifty-six, had every reason to abandon her trademark sense of humor. Soon after her diagnosis, she learned that her cancer had begun to spread from her breast, possibly to a lymph node, and she would need a mastectomy.

While every newly diagnosed patient probably feels alone and helpless, Cissy was truly alone, by conventional measures. Long divorced, childless, her parents both dead, and her closest relatives states away, she was entirely self-dependent. But helpless? That's where she showed the qualities that saw her (not to mention her friends) through the next several months.

That sense of humor was key.

After Cissy's combined mastectomy and reconstruction operation, when surgeons removed her right breast and pushed abdominal tissue under her skin to relocate it as new breast tissue, she examined the hip-to-hip incision across her lower body and said, in a morphine-induced slur, "I look like the circus act where they cut the woman in half—only they really did."

"But," she joked to her friends when she was more alert, "I got a free tummy tuck out of the deal."

Weeks later, when she was going to have a new nipple tattooed in place of her lost one, she told the doctor she would submit to a tattoo only if it said, "If you can read this, you're too close."

And Cissy was not alone. She had us, her circle of friends.

She didn't give any of us time to feel helpless, either. She gave us assignments.

Susan, her close friend, who would do anything to help but couldn't abide "anything gross," was given the task of contacting several family members after the operation, picking up groceries, getting nonmetal silverware in case the chemo left Cissy sensitive to metallic tastes in her mouth, and—most important—providing regular company.

I, less squeamish after having cared for a husband while he died of a fast-moving and cruel pancreatic cancer, got nursing duty. I changed bloody dressings in the days after that first massive surgery, cleaned up bed sheets, held her hand, and listened to her jokes.

A retired detective, one of many male friends who also stepped in to help, drove her to her chemo sessions.

Her hairdresser shaved Cissy's head, at her request, while another worker at the salon documented the scene in pictures. Taken in mid-shave, they show Cissy half-bald, tears standing in her eyes, laughing.

Other friends sent greeting cards and e-mails, provided food and comfort, and kept her in their prayers and meditations.

So it went for many months.

Cissy lost her hair but not her sense of humor. She got weaker of body but stronger of spirit. She balanced realism with hope. She survived, and she helped us all do the same.

That was four years ago, and every mammogram and MRI that Cissy has had since has come back clean. The lessons from her cancer battle, though, remain. The compassion and strength continue to fill up and spill over.

My mother inherited many of Cissy's hats and scarves when she was diagnosed with lymphoma last year. After my mother died in March, they were donated to a cancer center near her home, where other women can wear the same garments those two beloved women once wore.

Another friend was diagnosed with breast cancer this fall. The first thing we did was ask if we could throw her a hat party. (She declined our offer.)

Cissy continues to inspire the women who attended that first hat party four years ago. Many of us often revisit the day in our minds, reopening the gift Cissy gave to us: a sisterhood, whose membership might grow or decline with the passing of time and whose individual members might be frail or hearty, frightened or strong, but would be there whenever there was need. At the end of our group song, we knew in that moment that we were part of something larger than our separate selves—and far more powerful than fear, darkness, or a word falling from a doctor's tongue. And if that word came, thanks to Cissy, we would know what to do next.

—Kathie Ragsdale

Led by Love

A week after my first mammogram, I received an ominous-looking pink letter from the hospital telling me that my results required further evaluation. My husband, Tom, and I met with the radiologist and spent an hour looking at very large and very scary mammography pictures of my breasts. The radiologist talked a lot about statistics. I hate statistics. The next step was a visit to the surgeon.

Accompanied by our three-year-old son, Owen, Tom and I went to an intimidating complex of buildings owned by a medical corporation. We walked into a cavernous waiting room, which reminded me of a bank lobby with women stationed at regular intervals behind glass windows. I felt like everyone was watching me. *You're not that important,* I reminded myself when it occurred to me that the other people waiting might have their own reasons to be afraid.

The woman behind the glass window greeted us with a broad smile. "The doctor's running a half hour behind," she said.

"No problem," I replied. Why was I so polite? If we arrived thirty minutes late, we'd probably be asked to reschedule.

Tom managed to find one *TIME* magazine. *Someone, hopefully my insurance company, is paying this doctor $200 to tell me something I don't want to hear,* I groused, *and he can't subscribe to any magazines?*

Owen decided to practice his gardening skills on the pathetic-looking potted plants scattered around the room. *Doesn't anyone water them, for heaven's sake,* I thought. *They might actually perk up and make someone feel better.*

Owen wasn't interested in Tom's *TIME* nor in *Money*, the other magazine we found, so we spent most of our time saying, "No, Owen, don't climb on the furniture. No, Owen, don't do that. No, Owen. No, Owen." Then I realized I was asking a three-year-old to wait without being annoying and restless, something I seemed incapable of doing myself.

A woman called my name, and I trudged behind her until we reached an examining room.

Once inside, she asked, "How are you doing?" I know she was trying to be polite, but when I said, "Terrible," she looked surprised. *What did she expect me to say? I'm in a surgeon's office. I am pale and shaking. I am not doing well.*

A nurse took my history. My mother died thirteen years ago, and I haven't seen my father for eleven years. So, when she asked if there was any cancer in my family, the unsuspecting woman received more than a simple answer. "I don't know," I said. "My brother told me that our father might have prostate cancer, but I'm not sure, because my dad hasn't told me and my brother suffers from chronic depression and memory lapses." When she reached the questions about anxiety and depression, I started to cry. She didn't ask any more questions, just handed me a paper shirt, which ripped as soon as I put it on, and left.

The surgeon came in. *He needs a haircut and a new pair of shoes,* I thought.

He told me the mammogram showed a cluster of calcifications in my left breast. The radiologist never mentioned clusters. Clusters are bad. No one told me they're bad; I just knew. I decided there must be a course in medical school called Euphemisms 101. "Never say 'bad,'" the instructor tells his students. "Use words like 'concerned,' 'suspicious,' and 'potentially.'"

"The radiologist never mentioned clusters," I said.

"I work with Howard a lot, and sometimes it's just a question of different interpretations and semantics," the surgeon said.

I felt like telling him that he and Howard should get their stories straight. His next announcement pleased me even less.

"Apart from that one cluster I mentioned, your calcifications are very scattered, so I don't consider you a good candidate for the laser-guided biopsy. I'd recommend a regular biopsy."

I felt like an idiot. I didn't know how to respond to anything this man said. I was still waiting for someone to announce, "Wait, we made a terrible mistake," or better yet, "Wake up, Susan."

He stopped talking. Maybe he noticed I wasn't paying attention. The huge, full-color posters of diseased tissue surrounding me made it difficult to focus on his words. I looked at his glasses and wondered how long it had been since his last eye exam. I hoped he was happily married, and if he had children, they weren't giving him too much trouble. I wanted the man cutting into my body to be well-adjusted with perfect vision.

He started talking about statistics. My opinion of statistics hadn't changed since my visit to the radiologist. "Eighty-five to ninety percent of biopsies are benign," he said, "and of the remainder, ninety percent are curable." These numbers should have pleased me, but I couldn't help worrying about the percentage that didn't have a happy ending.

He scheduled my surgery for the following Friday. I was going to have outpatient surgery at the same hospital where Owen was born. Owen still nursed, but only on my right breast, the good, well-behaved breast. He consistently refused the left breast. *Why didn't he tell me something was up? "Hey Mom, this milk tastes like crap. Get it checked out."*

The surgeon said I'd be home by late afternoon. He recited a list of the possible risks involved, handed me a pen, and asked me to sign the permission form.

My hand began to tremble, and I paused.

"You know," he said, "the biopsy scar is nothing. You won't even be able to see it, but I can do the laser-guided biopsy if that's what you want."

My vision blurred. I blinked rapidly, but a few tears betrayed me and slid down my cheek. "I don't give a damn about my breasts," I said, "but I've got five incredible kids and a wonderful husband. I just want to get through this and be there for them."

The surgeon smiled. "I understand," he said quietly. He rested his hand on my arm for a few seconds, and suddenly, I didn't care if he ever got another haircut, and he could go barefoot if he wanted.

"I'll do my best," he said. "Do you have any more questions?"

"Just one," I said. "What would you tell me to do if I were your wife? Or your mother?

He answered without hesitation. "I'd tell you to have the regular biopsy."

"Okay," I said and signed the paper.

I wanted to tell him this wasn't the real me. I wanted to explain that I felt like one of those plastic containers I use for the breakfast cereal that I buy in economy-size bags. I always try to fit the whole bag in the container, but I can never quite do it. There's always a handful or so left over, but I keep trying to shake the container down so that all of it will fit. I usually end up spilling it. Leaving his office, I felt like my cereal was all over the floor. *How was I going to make it until Friday? How was I going to make it through the next five minutes?*

Back in the waiting room, Owen rushed up to me and hugged my knees. "I missed you, Mom."

Tom held me for a few minutes. I clung to him, and he whispered in my ear. "Everything's going to be all right, you know. I'll take care of you, and I'll make sure you get everything you need."

When I saw the love in my son's eyes and felt it in my husband's arms wrapped around me, I knew how I would get through this ordeal. Love that had brought me this far and love would help me go wherever life led me.

—*Susan B. Townsend*

The "M" Word

Mastectomy is not a bad word. I learned the "F" word when I was eight years old. I learned the "M" word at age thirty-six. My wife had breast cancer.

Back in 1966, breast cancer was still in the closet. Nobody famous jumped out and said, "Hey, everybody, I have breast cancer." No TV specials, no lapel pins. Hush! I was in for many surprises when that door creaked open.

Our children were growing up. The youngest, just starting first grade and a hanger-on, wanted no part of school and was my wife's third leg. We enjoyed reasonably good health, my wife, my three daughters, my son, and I. The usual ailments. I knew of no one who had cancer or who knew someone who had cancer. Our parents were alive and healthy. Lucky I guess.

My wife and I had returned from a dinner-dance affair. December was cold, but she warmed up the room. I will always remember that gold satin cocktail dress, a little risqué she thought; I loved it. It was the last time she wore it.

You sense when something is amiss. My wife wasn't singing. She always sang. She had a great voice. She fussed with the kids more. She gave me capricious looks that I misread. That night she asked me to check her breasts. Great! Not so great, I just confirmed she had a lump in her breast. The nightmare began . . . for her.

She knew more about her problem than she let on. Woman things. Why worry me needlessly, right? Sorry to say, I learned later what must have been going through her mind. She had discovered the lump weeks before, and smart gal that she was, she made doctors' appointments and had scheduled a visit with the surgeon. She asked a thousand questions, got all the data, had all the statistics. She was a loving wife and kept much of this from me. She gave me the sparse details she knew would satisfy my concern. Why should both of us worry? It wasn't time to worry yet; after all, the doctor assured us not to worry.

I regret to this day that I was not with her at the hospital. To minimize my concern, she hustled me off to work, a smile on her face. There was no need to worry. It was just another cold, bright January day, right?

I called. She was still in surgery. They must have started late. It was nothing; why worry, right?

The call came. The surgeon had a smooth, calming voice. He sounded like James Earl Jones. He was telling me all went well and she was in recovery. Then a long pause. I could hear hospital noises in the background.

"We had to do a radical mastectomy," he said.

Stupid me asked, "Did she lose her breast?"

More hospital noises.

"I'm afraid so," he said.

He should have said, "Of course, dummy. What the hell do you think?"

I learned a new word that day, at least the true meaning of the word.

On the drive to the hospital, I picked up my mother-in-law. She burst into tears when I used my newfound phrase. I was beginning to get a bad feeling. My usually talkative mother-in-law just sobbed and wiped off the rivers on her cheeks.

I stood motionless at my wife's bedside. Intravenous lines were dripping stuff into her veins. Half her body was wrapped in gauze; a tube draining a pinkish fluid into a bag hung from her bed. I remained speechless. I had never seen her so vulnerable, so helpless.

She was groggy from whatever painkiller they had given her, but her eyes were clear and they held mine in a worried stare. "Did I lose the breast?" she whispered. My vision blurred for a moment; I could taste the tears in the back of my throat. I swallowed hard and nodded. She closed her eyes and let the drugs remind her of a better day.

I remained at her bedside, waited and watched the tube that trickled with the pink stuff. I smiled at the nurse as she replaced the empty IV bag with a full one. My mind was drawing blanks. What could I possibly say to her when she awakened? Something humorous, witty? That was my norm when stressed. Gazing at my wife, pale, motionless, spots of blood on her cheek and neck they had not cleaned. No, humorous was out.

She began to stir and tried to wet her lips. Her eyes remained closed, but she called my name. I cradled her hand in mine. "I am here," I said. She squeezed my hand and tried to clear her throat with some effort. Her eyelids wrinkled and seemed to press tighter as she used to do when on a swing. "The bed is moving," she said and squeezed my hand tighter.

The nurse came in then, checked the IV and the drain. Rinsing a washcloth in cool water, she gently wiped my wife's face and neck. "That better, honey?" she asked. I thought so. It brought a little color to her face. She hadn't let go my hand and held it now to keep the room from spinning. Her eyes focused on me, and she repeated my name. Her gaze drifted to the mass of bandages and then back to me. I think I was weeping. I moved in close and kissed her cheek. "I love you," I said, and before she would ask, "The kids are fine." She patted my hand as if I were the one with the hurt.

My wife refused to leave the hospital "uneven," as she put it. She carefully padded her bra with hospital washcloths to even things out. It had to hurt. We left the hospital, her head held high.

I learned something new about my bride of fifteen years.

The first few days were awkward. The bandages still covered the operation. She had no idea how I would, or whether I could, handle what was to come.

She learned something new about her groom of fifteen years.

The surgeon held magic in his hands. All the horror stories that surfaced in the last few weeks became distant memories. When the bandages came off, there were no ugly scars or mutilated flesh, only a clean smooth surface that almost seemed natural. Easy for me to say; it wasn't my body.

Time passed. We talked about the operation, about cancer. I learn a lot about breast cancer, why my wife kept some things from me, and why she wanted to get things done and in order. After a while, we never gave statistics another thought.

I did remember some time later what I thought I might have said at her bedside that afternoon, you know, the funny line. I told her, about two years later, that it happened to be my favorite one. I do not want to repeat what she said.

Is there a happy ending here?

Oh, yes. We celebrated our fifty-seventh wedding anniversary in April.

—Joseph Pantatello

Only My Sisters Understand

My sisters are the only other human beings on this earth who, like me, become mind-numbingly paralyzed once a year. At mammogram time.

My husband, John, doesn't get it. Only my sisters understand.

The week before my mammogram, I become increasingly quiet. I wonder about the woman he'll take up with after I die of breast cancer. Oblivious to my suffering, he glares at the television screen as he spars with Bill O'Reilly.

One day, shortly before my yearly mammogram, the two of us walked companionably around the duck pond in the peaceful shadows of late afternoon.

"I want my brother Tom to give my eulogy," I suddenly blurted.

John stared at me.

"Just try to remember," I choked with emotion.

My husband shook his head in bewilderment.

But my sisters understand completely. Four of us have endured breast biopsies, and all five of us have meticulously planned our funerals. We have all pondered which women would fill in admirably as new wives and mothers to our husbands and children. They should be women who are wonderful and kind. But not *too* wonderful and kind. And not too cute. In fact, not cute at all.

My sisters and I have also made a pact. It is absolutely understood that if one of us is lying in an irreversible coma, it will be the responsibility of the others to sneak into the hospital room to discreetly remove any embarrassing facial hair.

We've pretty much got all our bases covered.

But only my sisters understand. And that's because of Mom.

We were just a young family when Mom discovered a lump in her breast. She was forty-five years old, beautiful and funny. The idea that anything like cancer could touch our big, happy family was unthinkable.

Three weeks later, Mom had an operation to biopsy the lump and woke up without a breast. That's the way it was done in 1976. The cancer had already spread, and Mom started radiation treatments immediately. There was no suggestion of chemotherapy at the time. But when it became clear that Mom's cancer had spread to her spine, the doctors removed her ovaries in a last-ditch attempt to slow its deadly progress. By that time, however, tiny tumors were already growing on her skull and pressing against her eyeball, robbing her of her vision.

She died in 1979, at the age of forty-eight.

Those three years were filled with heartbreak. My youngest brother, Jeff, was only four years old when Mom was diagnosed. During one of her hospital stays, I remember watching him crawl into my parents' bed one early morning. "Mommy," he sighed sleepily, clutching her pillow.

My sisters Deb and Mary, who were only teenagers, were suddenly thrust into the roles of cook and housekeeper. When my dad, bone-weary from dealing with my mother's illness and trying to care for ten kids, would walk through the door every night after work, my sisters would try to protect him. "Don't tell him Mom cried today," they'd warn my other siblings.

Mostly, though, I remember the end. When Mom died, my little brothers and sisters could hardly bear it. Huddled closely around our father, the ten of us shuffled up to our mother's casket at the funeral home to view her body for the first time. The four little ones suddenly collapsed onto Dad's lap, sobbing and clinging to him. I will never forget how he comforted them as tears streamed down his own face.

Cancer changed our family forever. It even broke us for a little while. But, ultimately, we learned to depend on each other. Even in our adult lives, my siblings and I are each others' best friends.

Still, of course, there have been times when I missed Mom so much it was a physical ache: on my wedding day, when I was pregnant with our first baby, when Dad died. And unexpected times, like when I was at my son's basketball game some years ago, sitting behind a woman about my age, who leaned over and whispered to her mother. They laughed and embraced, and I felt such a stab of longing.

Then I remember my family—my husband, John, my sons, my stepmom, my brothers and sisters, my in-laws. The whole dysfunctional clan. Cancer has taught me that what my dad always said is true: Family is everything.

And even though my sisters and I suffer temporary insanity every year when it's time for our mammograms, we know how lucky we are. There were no mammograms in 1976, no stereotactic biopsies, no chemotherapy, no drugs like tamoxifen to stop a deadly, aggressive cancer. It's because of Mom that my sisters and I remain ever vigilant, ready to stop the enemy.

Cancer taught us something else, too: It couldn't take Mom away. Not really. I see her in my sisters—in Deb's soothing voice, in Mary's expressive brown eyes, in Tern's quirky humor, in Caroline's adventurous spirit. And sometimes, when we all gather together—along with our lovely and tolerant stepmother, Kris, who is more sister than parent—the stories we share from those distant, happy days of our youth render us helpless. We laugh so hard it hurts. And in the middle of our hoots and cackling, I swear I hear the ghost of a familiar and much-loved giggle.

Cancer does not have the power to take our loved ones away. We just have to find them. I find Mom again every day—in precious photos, in the winter coat she once wore, in the way a small niece tilts her head just so. I find her in my brothers and sisters. They fill the aching void in my heart and show me what I think I've always known: Love is more powerful than anything . . . even cancer.

—*Cathy Howard*

Proceed

On a misty June morning I tell the boys. "Guys, I have some bad news," I say as we walk down Valley Road.

They stop, wait for me to catch up.

"I have breast cancer," I say.

Jack flashes me a steely look. He's the mathematician, the calculating one who likes order. Things aren't adding up.

"It's okay, though," I say. "I have good doctors taking care of me. I'll have to get sick to get better, but I'll be fine after that."

With lowered heads the boys hold a polite and deferential silence. We continue our walk.

"Jack, you wanna build a fort?" Joe asks.

"No, Joe," Jack replies. "We're playing baseball, remember?"

The phone rings in the second-floor guest bedroom.

"How are you feeling?" my sister Mary Jane asks.

The dam breaks.

"I don't know where to go, what to do. I can't move backward or forward. I'm trapped inside a body that I'm certain is killing me."

I go on.

My sister listens, empathetic and helpless.

Dim light filters through vinyl shades. Medical bills and old homework assignments hoard space on a cheap Polk Brothers table.

"And I hate this room," I add to make sure she understands the magnitude of my misery.

Sunny and seventy degrees, a gentle breeze blows in from Lake Michigan as we settle into our bleacher seats. My husband, Leo, passes down two Cokes, a beer, and a Wrigley Field visor to protect me from the sun.

The Cubs are leading in the ninth inning when Milwaukee's left-fielder cranks one over our heads onto Sheffield Avenue to bring in the winning run for the Brewers. Jack and Joe lean over the railing and watch Sammy Sosa shake his head in disgust.

The beer tastes bitter. I had started chemotherapy a week earlier.

I really do hate this room. We call it the guest room, but it's more like the "guest-office-what-should-we-do-with-this-old-crib" room.

Joe, my second grader, has been sleeping here for several weeks as a way of stepping out of his older brother, Jack's, shadow. The fifth grader on the top bunk—the guy with all the sports trophies—is unintentionally smothering Joe.

I want to fix up the room, create a place where Joe's personality will shine.

But I can't move forward.

My hair is falling out by the Fourth of July. Leo suggests that we shave my head rather than submit to the slow degradation of hair loss. I like the idea. Sinead O'Connor, here I come.

He sets up a lawn chair in the backyard and covers me with a white sheet. The boys take turns snipping off chunks of hair. After Leo buzzes my head, Joe says I look like Dr. Evil (from the *Austin Powers* films). I flip my wrist and bite my pinky. The boys laugh.

We watch the fireworks that evening from the Ford dealership on Northwest Highway. I wear my new wig.

The room suffocates me with its darkness and neglect. The old bachelor bed is shoved into the corner, swallowed up by a tattered, rust-colored blanket. Smiling blue bunnies peer from leftover wallpaper, taunting me with their permanence.

"I'm trapped," I whisper into the phone. My words hang in the air.

"You know," Mary Jane says slowly, carefully. "DIF works really well for removing wallpaper. Especially when you spray it on."

Deep beneath the layers of emptiness, I feel my sister's gentle nudge.

As I listen to her talk about wallpaper, I slowly move forward.

In August, between Adriamycin and Taxotere, we squeeze in a family vacation. We rent a house in Alabama, overlooking the Gulf of Mexico, with my brother-in-law's family.

I buy a toy musket for Joe at the gift shop in Fort Gaines. He crawls through tunnels and scampers up the brick stairs to the lookout tower. Pointing his gun toward Mobile Bay, he searches for the first sign of the Union fleet.

In the mornings, in a peach swim suit and a cream-colored turban, I watch shrimp boats drift by, serenaded by hungry seagulls. Laughter bounces off the water as Jack and Joe dangle from rafts with their cousins, waiting for the big wave.

The days peel by slowly.

I shiver on the sidelines, camouflaged between hat-clad moms on a cold October morning. The final dose of chemo bombards my insides.

Jack lifts his bruised body from the wet, gritty mess of a football field and lines up at his right-end position.

The quarterback drops back to pass, and Jack sees the opening. With the force of all eighty pounds, he drives into the back of the quarterback. The quarterback's shoulder pads and facemask bury into the earth, and the football jars loose.

A whistle pierces the air. Game over.

Another win for the Barrington Broncos Featherweights.

I hang up the phone and rise to the surging impulse inside of me. I'm drawn to a loose seam of wallpaper in the corner of the room. I peel off a long, satisfying swath. I move from panel to panel, stripping all that comes easily. I feel the wall, scrape with my fingernails, yank hard and viciously, over and over.

I'm learning the sad truth about wallpaper. The battle is not so much with the paper as it is with the glue underneath. Even with DIF, the paste comes off slowly, in tiny wads of goo. I scrape feverishly, angrily at one stubborn patch. As I gouge the wall, the razor pops out of my hand, flips upside-down, and slices my right wrist.

Blood oozes from the gash. The blade just misses my radial artery, so I am in no immediate danger. Leo wraps my hand tightly in strips from a pillow-case to staunch the bleeding.

The emergency room is busy on Saturday morning between football injuries and drug overdoses. I take a seat in the waiting room, relieved to be out of the house for awhile, away from my new arch enemy—wallpaper.

A well-dressed woman in the corner sobs loudly. At first, I think she is reacting to news of a loved one, but soon I realize she is the patient.

"Where am I?" she moans and covers her face with shaking hands.

Her husband tries to calm her, while the daughter calls her psychiatrist on the cell phone. The admitting nurse rolls her eyes as if to say, "Not her again."

But I feel her anguish. I have been to the edge.

It's been three and a half years since my diagnosis.

On a frigid February morning, with a cup of coffee in one hand, I climb the ladder to Joe's bunk bed.

"C'mon honey," I nudge. "We gotta work on those spelling words."

I place a soft pillow behind my moppy morning hair.

Joe slowly comes to life.

"Proceed," he mumbles. "P-r-o-c-e-e-d."

As he rattles off words, I sip my coffee and bask in the warmth of his room.

Frost on the outside of the window sparkles in the morning sun. A pirate ship poster wilts from the vapors of Joe's fish tank. My carefully planned navy-amber-white color scheme clashes with his Civil War map and his Kansas City Chiefs' pennant.

The gouge in the wall warms my heart, and I reach under the blanket to squeeze Joe's toes.

—Mary Ann O'Rourke

Remember Only the Laughter

"Humor will get you through this, Mags."

I couldn't believe what I was hearing. I'd just been diagnosed with breast cancer, and my best friend was telling me it was funny? I stared at her.

"You're angry with me for saying that, but you know I've been through it myself, and parts of it are funny. You'll see."

Although Anne had her mastectomy some years before we met, I guessed she'd been brave. That's the kind of person she is. But now she was expecting the same from me, and I wanted to smack her.

With two tumors in one breast, mastectomy was the only option. An MRI was scheduled to make sure there weren't tumors in the other breast. I was obliged to lie on my stomach while encased in a large plastic tube, my breasts poking through two holes in the bottom of the thing. Inelegant, embarrassing, and not funny. But I could pretend, and when I described the procedure to friends later, I had them doubled over with mirth.

No tumors were discovered in the other breast, but what if they developed later? No way was I going through this twice.

"I want a matching set," I told Dr. V., my plastic surgeon.

"We can take some of your abdominal tissue and create two breasts. I can tell you're a candidate for doing it that way," he said, his eyes measuring the girth of my stomach. "You'll get a tummy-tuck out of it."

Maybe things weren't quite so black after all.

"Did he show you pictures of boobs?" Anne asked.

"Yeah, he gave me a folder, but I didn't really look at it."

"Then how're you gonna decide what size you want?"

"I assumed one size fits all."

"You'd better call him and discuss what you want."

"I'm not talking about it on the phone."

I wanted perky, but how was I going to get that across? It was seven days before the surgery, and that's what was on my mind. Not whether I'd survive surgery, not whether I'd be in terrible pain, and not whether the cancer would recur in other organs. No, I worried about perky versus non-perky breasts. Hadn't Dr. V.'s eyes positively gleamed as he surveyed the extent of my tummy flab? I couldn't face calling him, but I'd bring up the subject just before going into surgery.

I was in pre-op, looking through the pink haze resulting from relaxant meds. Dr. V. stopped by, patted me on the arm, smile firmly in place.

"You're going to be fine," he said.

Thoroughly pleased with myself, I grinned back, "Dr. V., I want you to think Audrey Hepburn rather than Dolly Parton."

"Our resources are limited," he said.

We should be on the comedy circuit, the doc and I.

Whether the ten-hour surgery was amusing or not, I have no way of knowing. Perhaps there was black humor to cut the tension. Isn't that what they did on M*A*S*H? Whatever, I didn't get to share in any laughs.

Things were most definitely not funny when I awoke; nor were they for the next several weeks. But as I began to feel human again I realized there was an upside to the situation. Friends came bearing food and flowers; they called on the phone and were tireless in their efforts to cheer me. I ruminated about how I could get the same service once I was healthy.

"Okay, so now the bandages are off. Are they perky?" Anne said.

"They look like pancakes. Wanna take a look?" I pulled up my shirt, modesty being a thing of the past.

"Hmm . . . They don't look like pancakes."

"What do they look like then?"

"Well, with those circular scars around each of them, they remind me of a Panda's face. When you get the nipples done later, they'll be the Panda's eyes."

"You're a real comfort." I forced a laugh.

"Sorry, I can see you don't think it's funny. But the scars will fade, Mags, you know they will."

"Maybe. But forget the nipples. I've had enough."

"Come on, you can't leave the job half done."

Six months later, Dr. V. said we should now replace my nipples.

"I couldn't care less about nipples. But earlier you suggested we might do some liposuction under my arms. Can we still do that?"

"Sure."

"Will it be covered by insurance?"

"Well, if you have nipples reconstructed, I could do the liposuction at the same time. That way it will look like fine-tuning of the previous surgery rather than a cosmetic procedure."

"You've got a deal."

He told me I'd have nipples, but he didn't mention they'd be the size of door-stops. And he didn't tell me they'd be bristly. He'd said nothing about bristly nipples. That's what I ended up with—nipples with a five o'clock shadow.

"They'll shrink to a normal size," reassured Dr. V. "And you'll soon shed the stitches."

For weeks, until the stitches fell out, I had an uncontrollable urge to play with the tiny black nylon tufts that sprang from each breast. I tried not to do this in public.

And this time I did not have to pretend it was funny. It was funny. Hysterical, in fact.

Anne had been right. Humor, feigned or otherwise, had gotten me through.

—*Margaret B. Davidson*

Pieta's Promise

When Michelangelo, the great sixteenth-century Italian artist and sculptor, began a new Pieta, he started with an unhewn boulder, an indiscreet block of rock. He stood staring at the stone for hours, until he saw an image, a form, emerge from the rock. An arm, a hand, or a knee would protrude from the face of the stone, begging to be set free. Then, he began to chip and carve, releasing the entity that lay trapped inside.

Sometimes his work ended before the full figure was carved. The Academy Gallery in Florence, Italy, where the statue of David resides, contains multiple Pietas that appear to be unfinished. To Michelangelo, however, as soon as the figure was released, the sculpture was complete. It did not matter to him if there were only an arm, half a face, or a portion of the Holy Mother's body distinguished from the rock.

From September 2001 through September 2003, I launched a search for my personal Pieta. Diagnosed with breast cancer one week after the September 11 terrorist attacks on the United States, I underwent a bilateral mastectomy and subsequent reconstruction, a retina detachment and lens replacement in my left eye, and a complete hysterectomy. Like Michelangelo's artistic essence, it was only after my surgeries that I, too, began to be fully realized. With each knife's paring away of flesh, with each organ that was removed, I came closer to understanding who I am and what I wanted out of life. My options were narrowed, finely tuned to be clear choices and not compromises.

In addition to the surgeon's excisions, Life carved away more of my heart as my closest friend died of breast cancer after an eight-year battle. Seven months after my own cancer diagnosis, my mother died of lung cancer, succumbing to a valiant fight with an inoperable tumor and a failing heart interminably weakened by a single round of chemotherapy.

These assaults on my body, heart, and mind took their toll on me in innumerable ways, many of which are surfacing only now as the days between my cancer and me increase. Mostly, though, it is my relationship with my eight-year-old daughter that gives me perspective, gives me hope and motivation to assimilate these experiences carefully and fully. As she grows into a young person of talent and choices, I consider carefully how to guide her in her metamorphoses. How do I instill or help direct my daughter's identity? Will she grow naturally toward a stable, healthy future? Will her experiences cause her to cast off unwanted principles and behaviors? I search for more meaning in my life—not reasons why, but lessons in my every day to keep me on track with my daughter and with myself.

My responsibility as a role model for my daughter has become my prime directive in my post-cancer years. How I respond to monumental crises or just the simple ones she faces in third grade show her ways to live her life. If I react as a victim, she will learn to be a victim. If I act with courage, tenacity, and confidence, her mirror will, hopefully, reflect that too.

That does not mean we walk through life holding hands in denial. While the personal power and insight I have gained from my experience is undeniable, I cannot ignore the other side of this survival equation. In other words, I must embrace the losses I've endured as well as the strengths I've gained. The loss of my organs, the loss of my youth, the loss of my marriage, the loss of my mother, my final living parent. The loss of my emotional blindness that kept me from facing the sickly comforting emptiness left from a horrific childhood. The loss of my Innocent who looked forward to Christmas and dreamed the Knight was on his way.

The loss of the Blind Believer who knew that God and Jesus would make everything okay eventually. The loss of the Achiever who knew she could sit at the helm of any ship in the corporate harbor. She believed she could win, and the heady sensation of winning was everything. Those aspects of me, aspects of my Self, are gone. They have transformed into something stronger. And wiser. And braver. But, intrinsically sadder now, I mourn the losses nonetheless.

I have gained much during my journey. I have learned how to live fully. I have finally learned the importance of being a mother for my beautiful child, above all else. I have begun an autopsy on what's left of my Self, so I can expose my Essence, my true Spirit and Heart, which lay buried for so many years. I have learned to sing and laugh and dance and to say what I think without worrying that it might cause someone to leave me.

Some would say that it took tremendous courage to have my breasts lopped off and to elect to have three reconstructive surgeries to rebuild my chest. The complete hysterectomy would have put other, weaker women over the edge. "You are so brave," women have said to me over and over again.

Surviving is not coming out on the other side and resurrecting like some triumphant Phoenix, singed and dark from the flames but flying nevertheless. The experience of those difficult months hangs around me like an invisible cawl. At times, it is a victim's cloak, deep, swirling, purple velvet that both protects and insulates me from the rest of the world. But as the days pass I find myself rising beyond the tethers of the traumas themselves. The memories that caused me so much sadness and worked to redefine me are fading into the past. They are becoming the story I tell the long-lost friend who asks, "How have you been?" The words tumble out easily, and I am even managing to weave in a few jokes from time to time. Interesting, how humor emerges as the pain dissipates.

I work to assimilate my experience as a survivor into my everyday life. I want to return to my pre-surgery self, but that is impossible. It would be like wishing a shooting star could return to its original orbit, its celestial starting point in the sky. At the end of its travels, the star has become something else long before the shimmer of its tail fades. It is no longer the star or the racing meteor. It is a dimming glimmer, and as it fades, all that remains is the memory of its heavenly scar, even as the incision across the sky quiets to nothing.

It is the same with the scars on my breasts, abdomen, and heart. They are the evidence of my growth, my path to the wise woman I am today. Without them to remind me as I step out of the shower each morning and catch a glimpse of myself in the steamy mirror, I might forget how hard I have worked ... how far I have come. I might assimilate the sacrifices too completely, seeing only the monarch butterfly in its post-pupae glory. The awesome metamorphosis would be lost.

As effortless as the flight of a butterfly might seem as it lights from flower to flower, its emergence from the cocoon is never easy. There must be blood and tearing tissue and searing pain as the determined insect rips open the casing and forces her way outside. Then, as the pain subsides, she breathes her first sweet air and takes her first shaky steps toward the sun. After her birthing struggle has subsided, she is ready for the world, taking every opportunity to drink in the delicious nectar Life provides.

Like the tentative butterfly, I, too, am emerging from my cocoon. I have broken through to see the sun and to breathe free. However, unlike the butterfly, I hope to remember every step of my struggle, every painful choice and subsequent achievement. Only with the benchmark of painful memory can I hold onto the awesomeness of who I am today. I am my own Pieta, reaching out from the stone that held me tight before the chiseling began. And while my daughter watches my emergence from the sidelines of her own life, I pray she will embrace the graces of survival, holding them in reserve for a day when she will inevitably need them.

—*Virginia Hardee Silverman*

Hidden Treasures

I was diagnosed with advanced stage-three breast cancer at age forty-four. My children were teenagers at the time, so I woke every morning to images of all the important events in their lives I might miss. One day I was out shopping when I spotted a beautiful carousel that played "The Wedding March." My youngest daughter collected carousels. As I drove home, I thought what a lovely wedding present that would be, so I turned around and went back to buy it. Fighting back tears, wondering whether I would be there to share her special day, I took my precious gift home and hid it in the camelback trunk that had belonged to my grandmother.

I lay awake at night trying to decide what to buy for my oldest daughter and my son for their future weddings. I wanted the gifts to be keepsakes that came from the heart. Several weeks later, a *Duck's*

Unlimited waterfowl magazine arrived in the mail. I glanced through it and found a hand-painted collector's stein. I immediately placed my order, pleased that I had found just the right gift for my son, an avid hunter. When the package arrived, I stuck it under my bed and waited until the coast was clear for me to scrutinize the present. The signed and numbered mug passed inspection, so I gently laid it in the trunk next to the carousel.

Keeping secrets has always been hard for me to do, but this was something I wasn't willing to share even with my best friend, my husband. I was afraid my loved ones would interpret the gifts as a sign I had given up. I intended to go to war against cancer with a take-no-prisoners attitude. However, purchasing the presents gave me peace of mind, knowing that my children would feel their mother's love reaching out to them in the event things didn't turn out as I hoped.

Several weeks later, my sisters and I cycled twenty miles on the Katy Trail. Then we visited the historic section of St. Charles, Missouri, known for its antique shops and luscious restaurants. While my sisters casually browsed, I barreled through stores like Patton marching through Germany. Walking up the narrow wooden steps to the second level of a specialty shop, I spotted a beautiful Victorian jewelry box adorned with pearls, porcelain flowers, and glass beads with a picture of a lovely bride gracing the lid. Perfect! When the saleswoman opened it, I was serenaded by the sweet melody of "Love Story." Wedding present number three!

As I was paying for my treasure, my sisters walked up behind me, saying, "There she is!"

They thought I had left the store and had been trying to track me down. My face turned red as I tried to hurry the clerk along, but my sisters wanted to see my find. I sheepishly handed it over. They both marveled at its beauty.

"There's not a wedding coming up, is there?" a sister asked.

Not usually at a loss for words, I tried to come up with a witty reply but failed. We left the store and sat down on a nearby bench, where I blabbed my secret. There wasn't a dry eye as I told them about the keepsakes I had purchased for a future that might not include me. I emphasized that I wasn't about to quit the fight, but I wanted everything in order, just in case. I swore my sisters to secrecy, admitting that I also found a gift for my youngest daughter's high school graduation. I had one more confession to make: The musical bootie, train, and pink princess planters I had received from our grandparents to welcome my babies were also tucked inside the trunk. I added a note to fill with flowers and deliver to the hospital when my grandchildren were born. Although I was determined to be at these special occasions in person, as a precaution, my love letters were placed inside each tenderly wrapped present.

With the gifts all nestled in Grandma's trunk, I could now concentrate on winning my battle with cancer.

Twelve years have passed since my initial diagnosis. Grandma's trunk is empty. All the presents have been personally delivered. The weddings were beautiful, and yes, I cried, but they were tears of joy. My eight grandchildren are the most precious gifts I could ever ask for. It's too soon to buy special keepsakes for their graduations and weddings. Besides, I plan to present them myself.

—Alice Muschany

Location, Location, Location

My heart skips a beat as I sign for the registered letter I've been expecting. I set the letter on the kitchen island and turn to make my morning cappuccino, needing a moment to calm down and to prepare myself for what I was about to read.

It is an unusually warm October day in Manitoba, and a memory warms my heart as I reach for the yellow cup with the brightly colored design. We have only two of these cups. When my husband and I saw them in the store, they reminded us of a village in Italy we had visited earlier that year, and we had to have them. Now, it brings back memories of us sitting outside a cafe overlooking the Mediterranean, drinking cappuccinos capped in white foam with sailboats drawn in chocolate syrup.

While I sip from the cup, the unopened letter in front of me brings forth other, less pleasant memories.

My journey leading to this letter began with a mastectomy, followed by chemo and radiation, and chemo again three years later. I've undergone thirteen ultrasounds, four biopsies, four CT scans, two Muggas, five bone scans, and two PET scans. Some months, my white blood counts went dangerously low; not wanting to contract infections, my work and social life were put on the back burner.

My husband has supported me through every procedure and through every decision that had to be made. With each diagnosis, we have prepared for the worst and hoped for the best. We have discussed my possible death and him going on without me. I've told him my worst thoughts and fears, and he has listened, sometimes with tears in his eyes.

The way has been tough at times, but it's also been highlighted by silver linings. The first set of chemo ended my twenty-five years of debilitating migraines. I have good medical coverage, so finances have never been a concern. I've received more gifts, cards, and flowers than one person could ever deserve; I often reread with gratitude the kind thoughts that were sent my way. In the seven years since my initial diagnosis of breast cancer, I have developed new friendships, had more time for quilting, and had less stress than I've had for years.

That said, the events of the past year have really tested my mettle. The breast cancer returned for a third time in the same left side of my chest. Radiation was the plan of attack this go around, and once again, I prepared myself emotionally and mentally for the treatments.

As usual, the therapy began with an appointment to mark the area to be radiated. I lay attentively on the hard table, thinking about a close coworker who had lost a battle with cancer and whose funeral I had attended just one week earlier. I could not help but think about my mortality. The radiation oncologist quickly looked at my file and then as quickly began marking my left chest. I could not be sure, but I thought the ultrasound had identified the lump a bit lower and farther to the left. I mentioned this to the oncologist, but he ignored me and kept marking.

Throughout the twenty-five treatments, I could not get the thought out of my mind that they were radiating the wrong area. I made comments to my husband, friends, medical staff, and even the technicians who administered the treatments. "Are you sure you are treating the right area?" I asked a number of times. No one ever took my comments seriously. On the last day of treatments, my husband took me out for a wonderful lunch to celebrate. It was time to focus on recuperating and moving on.

We did just that, and life was good . . . until two months later, when I went in for a follow-up ultrasound. Upon completing his task, the technician said, "I am sorry to give you this bad news, but the tumor was never radiated." My mind whirled. I didn't know what to say at first, but then I recovered enough from the shock to ask the technician to mark the correct location of the tumor. The circular burn on my left chest from the radiation was not even close to the mark he made.

I knew it! I was right all along! I thought as I walked down the hall, feeling disoriented and disconnected from my body. Though I'd known it deep inside all along, I was still stunned by what I had just seen and heard. And scared. And angry. A wild mix of emotions and thoughts raced through me. My trust in the medical system fell apart, and my heart sank.

Fortunately, the ultrasound clinic was in the same building as the cancer center, where the staff had been so supportive of me throughout the years. So I immediately went to meet with the cancer liaison there. I explained what I had just been told and then broke down, something I had never done in the past. I cried, yelled, cried, yelled, and cried some more. They calmly listened to me vent for more than an hour. They said they would make calls.

Two days later, my husband and I were sitting with a new radiation oncologist. He set the wheels in motion for correct treatments to start immediately. Another six weeks of radiation followed.

I had worked hard to remain positive throughout my seven-year ordeal with breast cancer. But when my suspicions were confirmed and I knew I'd lost precious time going through a difficult procedure that had no effect on the growing tumor, my glass suddenly became half empty for the first time.

Now what? The tumor had grown. Had the cancer spread, too? Was I going to die this time? How could a doctor play with my life like that? I was so scared and mad and sad. Lawyers advised me that suing would be futile. But I needed to do something constructive to ensure this would not happen to someone else. Something good had to come of this.

So I started writing letters. I wrote to the College of Physician and Surgeons of my province. I wrote to the facility where the error had occurred. I made requests for investigations. I spent hours at the computer, compiling pages of tediously organized information.

It was fortunate that, from the time I was first diagnosed, I had been keeping a detailed daily journal of my experiences—including the events and discussions that took place between me and the clinicians who administered care, consultation, and treatment. I'd also saved annotated appointment calendars, which helped me with dates and facts. My letters of complaint included a wealth of facts along with photos of my chest and all my medical records.

Although I was still upset, my stress began to lessen, my anger slowly turned to determination, and my emotional strength began to return. I spent the next year meeting and communicating with both agencies, and they have kept me informed of their progress with the investigation.

It's been fifteen months since I sent in my requests for investigations. The letter in front of me is the complaint committee's final findings. I'd already received a response from one investigation, telling me that the radiation treatments had "met acceptable standards of care." I'd hoped for more. What would today's letter say?

I glance at the envelope, but continue to sip the cappuccino from my yellow cup as I look out the kitchen window, watching leaves fall softly onto the lawn, and think about the changes this year has brought. After the harrowing events of the past year and with a second round of radiation treatments over, I'd decided it was time to retire. Life was good once again, but I felt I needed something just for me. One day a quilting friend mentioned she was going to the gym. I decided exercise might be a positive activity for me. I had become sedentary, gained twenty-five pounds, and lost what little strength I'd had prior to the recurrence of the breast cancer. Exercise would be my new job; I bought a year's membership at the gym and scheduled workouts for three days a week.

The staff at the gym developed a program for me to follow, and on the first day it became obvious that they had overestimated my abilities. Five minutes, not twenty, on the elliptical trainer and three-pound weights, not five, seemed to be the most I could handle. It was hard work, but I kept at it. After the first few months, my clothing began to feel loose. I could also handle longer walks and keep up with my husband on our recreational bike rides and hikes.

Nine months later, I use ten-pound weights and spend an hour on the elliptical trainer, still working out at the gym regularly. Having lost both inches and pounds, I like what I see in the mirror and enjoy shopping for clothes again. I eat breakfast daily, which I had not done most of my adult life, and I feel and look better than I have in ten years. More important, losing the extra weight, eating a lean diet, and exercising regularly helps to decrease my chances of breast cancer returning.

As I look at the envelope, I realize that it really doesn't matter now what the letter says. I have taken control of my life, and that is what is important.

Yes, it has been a difficult year, but in the end, it was a good one. My husband has been my devoted partner every day, loving me even when I am at my lowest. My daughter, my family, and my friends have listened to my saga and have continually reminded me of how positive I am, even when I didn't feel the least bit optimistic. I am also grateful, of course, to the medical professionals who listened and provided excellent advice, care, and support when I needed it most—especially my new radiation oncologist, one of the few medical professionals who acknowledged that a terrible error had been made.

Oh, yes . . . the letter. You are probably wondering what it says. Well, I will open it later today when my husband gets home. In fact, I think I will let him read it first. I have found a way to move on; maybe the letter will help him to do the same.

—Sally Gilchrest-Unrau

Postscript: The letter concluded that, although the doctor may have treated a legitimate tumor, he had missed the originally identified tumor. He received a letter of reprimand along with recommendations for improving communication and coordination among the different clinicians and facilities involved on each case.

Well Wishes

Today my husband and I were shopping in the mall, and we went into a card store on kind of a lark. We sometimes do this—stop and buy cards for family and friends and others in need, and then end up spending much more money than we intended. We had a few people in mind this time, and the person at the top of our list was Dan, my husband's brother. Last year, Dan was diagnosed with lung cancer and went through surgery and chemo. It has since metastasized. He had brain surgery a couple months ago to remove two spots, and he is now in the midst of intensive chemotherapy, again. He is not feeling well. And I know, just like I know that leaves are green and the sky is blue, that Dan's prospects for a complete recovery are not at all certain. I know this because I've known a number of people with the same diagnosis, and I myself have had cancer too. So picking out a card for Dan was an important task for both my husband and me.

As we scanned through the get well cards, I came across a section of cancer cards. I'd never seen cancer cards before. Here, I thought, we might find what we need. But as I opened up each of the cards and read the contents, I was astounded at how bad they were, how much I would not have wanted to get any of these cards when I was recovering myself. I couldn't find a single one that I would give to anyone with a diagnosis of cancer. There were "Sorry you have cancer" cards and "Gee, you're so strong" cards and "You've been cancer-free for one year!" cards. Ouch.

Actually, they made me angry. Five years ago when I was being treated for breast cancer, I wasn't feeling sorry for myself and I didn't need to hear that message. I sure wasn't feeling strong. Indeed, I felt like I was barely getting through each day, putting one foot in front of the other, and I didn't want to have to be strong. Did I have a choice? No. I just did it. And the whole cancer-free thing—boy, there were a bunch of cards with that message on them. Excuse me, but can anyone ever say we are cancer-free? Even those who have never even been diagnosed with it? To me, that statement was a subtle denial of the enormity of the situation for the person to whom the card was to be addressed. It felt like being touched by someone but only after they had put on latex gloves first.

Then it hit me like an intense wave, unsteadying me and making me so close to nauseous that I wanted to find a chair to sit down in. I realized that I know something quite intimately that the authors of these cards do not—something no one but those who have been confronted with their own looming mortality could possibly comprehend. I know that life is tenuous, that there are no guarantees. I know this deep down to my very bones, because I have tasted it and the taste clings to my mouth. I cannot rid myself of it. My reality cannot be skirted or evaded as if it were the object of one of these off-the-shelf get well cards.

When I was recovering from surgery and going through chemo, many people at work would come into my office—some to chat, some to ask questions, some to express their concern or desire to help. Everyone had a different way of doing it. But one man I worked with rather closely never stopped to say hi, never said a word about what I was going through. For a long time, I was kind of hurt by this. I thought his behavior strange, thought that perhaps he was an insensitive man. But for the next three years running, each time I organized a breast cancer walk, he was one of the first to sign up. Not only did he sign up, he also made a generous contribution and brought all of his daughters to the walk. So I have learned that different people handle things differently, and I think they show support in the best way they can.

I learned something else, too. In the past, when someone I knew was sick or sad, I never knew what to say, and to avoid saying the wrong thing, because I am basically shy, I would often say nothing. Those people who walked into my office may have had the same worries, but they had braved past them. And their visits comforted me. In a way, their visits made me feel like I was still one of them, even though I didn't even feel like me anymore. Wearing a wig, having had my left breast removed, having a tenth of the energy I used to, and being faced with many more treatments, I felt like my world had been ripped away from me. I needed to find a new world, a new place of comfort, and they helped me do just that. I learned that it's actually hard to say the wrong thing. What matters is that you say something. So, perhaps I should forgive the card writers, because they are just trying to relay a message of caring in the best way they can.

Still, my husband and I were left with what kind of card to get Dan. The only one my husband felt comfortable with was a humorous one. The cover had a pretty poetic message on it, and then, on the inside it said something like, "I think you'd have to be on medication to understand that. So, do you get it?" It was funny and touching at the same time, in a guy sort of way.

When we got home, my husband sat down at the dining room table and pondered for a while over what he would write in the card. He ended up writing a pretty sentimental message, belying his true thoughts and intentions. His message, really, was that he thinks about his brother a lot and that he loves him.

What do I wish for Dan? I wish for him the things that I'd wished for myself five years ago. I wish for him days when he feels like he can handle it. I wish for him many moments of being simply over-taken by the beauty of life around him—the leaves glistening in the sun, the laughter of his children, the delicate touch of an Indian summer breeze. I wish for him to know how much he is loved and cared for by his family and friends. I, of course, also wish for him a complete and total physical healing and that he never has to deal with this again.

Whatever Dan's future holds, I hope most fervently of all that he can find a place of peace amidst it all. I know it is hard to do, that this place can be elusive. But I also know—like I know fish swim and the ocean is wide—that it is within reach and that each of us can find this place of peace within ourselves.

—*Jennifer Swanson*

I Went and Washed That Hair Right Offa My Head

I had trouble concentrating at work the day my hair was scheduled to fall out.

My oncologist had told me my hair would begin to loosen a few days after the first dose of Adriamycin and then fall out quickly over the next few days. It was now two weeks since I'd started chemotherapy and three months after my breast cancer diagnosis. For the last ten days, I had been anxiously tugging at my hair, but it still seemed solidly attached.

"Maybe it won't happen to you," I told my reflection in the mirror that morning as I peered anxiously at my hairline. "You haven't gotten nauseous; you have no mouth sores, no fever, no fatigue, and none of the other side effects they predicted. Maybe you won't get this one either."

Despite the morning mirror bravado, there was no
way the highly toxic Adriamycin in my bloodstream

would miss those unsuspecting hair cells. I pictured the red liquid swooping upon them like a tidal wave, sending them crashing against a rocky beach, where they would dry out and wither away. I shuddered and stopped the image playing in my mind.

As I got dressed I noticed a few strands of hair on my shirt after I pulled it over my head. I did some gentle tugging again, but the hair still seemed solidly attached. Nevertheless, I was convinced that my hair was going to fall off that day, all at once, in a giant clump. I still hadn't bought a wig, so I packed a scarf in my purse to ensure I'd have some head cover.

By the time I got in to the office, a new image was playing in my head, like a B movie: "Maria Goes Bald in the Flash of an Eye." There I was, I envisioned, sitting in a meeting with several other people, and when I stood up from the table to make a presentation, my hair stayed behind. It hung suspended in midair for a few seconds as all eyes moved up to stare at it. Then it fell to the floor with a gentle tinkling sound, the kind of sound Charlie Brown's Christmas tree made when all the needles fell off. All eyes then moved to my naked head as it glistened in the afternoon sun.

I didn't even have any meetings that day, and I spent the entire afternoon sitting at my desk doing paperwork, occasionally tugging at my hair.

The next day I bought a wig. The salon didn't have the color I wanted, but they assured me they could get one in two days, well before I lost my hair. They also gave me a booklet with suggestions about different ways to prolong the life of your hair after chemo. One recommendation was to cut your hair short so that brushing didn't pull any more of it out. That made sense, so I scheduled an appointment with my hairdresser for that afternoon.

"Cut it very short," I told him as he stood over me with his scissors. "It's the last haircut you'll be giving me for about a year, so make it a good one."

My friend Dick drove me to my second chemo appointment and told me his wife suggested that he and another colleague shave their own heads as a gesture of support and friendship. Then she reconsidered, concerned that perhaps their hair might not grow back. I told them it was a very kind thought but there were enough bald-headed men around campus to form a large support group, and they had already been sending me suggestions on how to care for a hairless head.

The doctor and nurse were surprised to see that I still had my hair. Most patients had lost it by their second treatment.

"It's stubborn, like me," I told them.

I wore my wig to work the next week, even though I still had my own hair. Everyone said,

"You got a haircut; it looks nice." I laughed. Then they'd step back, look again, and say, "Oh, you mean it's the wig? Wow, it looks so real." The wig felt a bit itchy by the end of the day, so it was a relief to take it off when I got home. The next day I wore a scarf, and the day after that I wore a hat. Then I left all the headgear at home and wore my new short haircut. By then, people couldn't tell which was which.

"Is that your hair?" my assistant asked one day.

"Look, it's all my hair," I told her. "Some is home-grown, some is store-bought, but it's all mine."

No one could understand why my hair was lasting so long. My sister suggested I shave my head so I wouldn't have to prolong the agony of watching it fall out. "Not a chance," I told her. "It's not ready to go, so I'm keeping it as long as it wants to stay."

By the fourth week, it was loosening and I could see more evidence of that each day. I noticed hair in my underpants—it hadn't occurred to me that it could fall out of places other than my head—and there were more and more hairs on my shirt each day. I still tugged at it but more gently. It wasn't coming out in the clumps I'd dreaded, so that made me feel it was worth preserving. It was short enough that I didn't need to brush it, and I didn't have to wash it often, so that prolonged its lifespan.

"Why don't you just stop washing it altogether," my sister suggested. "That way it could last for months."

"It might," I told her, "but people would avoid me for months."

Windy days gave new meaning to the wind-blown look. When I arrived at work one morning, my hair was standing straight up. By the time I got home, it had blown over to the left side.

Finally, by the fifth of July, I felt ready for a final separation. I'd visited friends earlier that day and took off my baseball cap to show off my still solid groundcover, windblown, matted, and grubby, yet still very present.

"I don't know what you're concerned about," John said, taking off his baseball cap and rubbing his retreating hairline. "You have a lot more than I do."

But it was shedding more and more, and my white shirt looked as though it were sprouting hair on the shoulders.

That's it, I decided on the drive home. *I can't be bothered hanging on to it any more. I made my point, I kept the hair longer than anyone thought I would, and I'm tired of waiting.*

I stopped at the grocery store and bought some Dove ice cream bars, then went home, ate one of them, relaxed, and took a few deep breaths. I dug out a CD of Irish music and began to sing along with "While the Humor Is on Me Now" as I stripped down to my underwear. I didn't want to take a shower, because I thought it would be too creepy to get the hair all over me, so I took down the shower hose, knelt on the bathroom floor, leaned over the edge of the tub, and shampooed up a storm.

"I must get rid of this hair while the humor is on me now," I warbled as I rubbed. And rubbed. And rubbed. I couldn't believe how much hair was still left. It had been shedding for weeks, I'd had a significant haircut, and look how much was left. It kept coming off. The water started backing up in the tub, so I changed tunes.

"I'm gonna wash that hair right offa my head and watch it clog the drain," I sang in my best Mary Martin impression as I scooped a handful of hair out of the drain and flung it in the trash. I had to do that twice more before it felt like it was all gone.

I grabbed a towel to dry my hair and then realized I had none to dry. But I wrapped the towel around my head as I passed the mirror, not quite ready to view my new look.

What if I have an ugly skull? I wondered. My head had always felt a little lumpy, and there was that flat spot on the crown. *Does everyone have that or is it just me? What if I don't recognize myself? What if I look so different without hair that I don't even look familiar to me?* Never mind that I'd had a hundred different hairstyles and many shades of color over the years.

I had another Dove bar as I pondered these matters and worked up the nerve to look at my head. Fortified with sugar and courage, and while the humor was still on me, I walked down the hall to my vanity table and slowly, slowly inched my way in front of the mirror.

I stared back at myself, just as I had all those other times I'd sat in front of the mirror. It was me—recognizable, a bit different, but still me. The shape of my head seemed normal; none of the lumps were visible, although I could still feel them, and I couldn't even see the flat spot on my crown.

And there was something else familiar about my look. I reminded me of someone else. Who was it? I finally decided I looked a bit like Bruce Willis. Not so bad, I thought. He's a tough guy.

Two days later, the mail brought me a flyer advertising Dolly Parton wigs. I was about to throw it away when something caught my eye. Her signature looked familiar. I grabbed my wig and turned it inside out to look at the label. It had the same signature. I had bought a Dolly Parton wig.

"I love my wigs," said Dolly's flyer. "They let me change my look in seconds."

"Me, too," I told Dolly's flyer. "Especially when I take it off!"

The process of losing my hair largely reflected my overall cancer experience, initially fearful and filled with dread, yet ultimately manageable and filled with surprising humor. During the twelve months I spent in treatment, my father, my aunt, and my uncle were all diagnosed with cancer, and my father died ten weeks after his diagnosis. There were times when I felt surrounded by the disease, but mostly I kept working, maintained my routine, and sometimes didn't think about cancer for days at a time, despite the ever-present reminders. My hair started to grow back shortly after my fourth dose of chemo, and three months later I packed away the wig.

That was more than ten years ago. I still have physical reminders of the cancer—two scars, some extra pounds, a pill I take each morning, and the wig lying on a shelf in my closet. But the psychological reminders are more enduring—the courage to face the ordeal, the ability to laugh through the occasional tears, and the survivor spirit I always had but didn't fully realize before that March day in 1997, when the doctor told me I had cancer.

—Maria S. Judge

Good to Go

I take a deep breath and calm the quiver in my throat before I call to my husband and lover of thirty-five years. "Honey?"

"Yes."

I pull my shoulders back; my spine straightens and my chest expands. "Do you notice the size difference in my breasts? The necklines are so much lower than last year. There seems to be so much cleavage."

"Let me get my bifocals." He reaches for his glasses on the dresser, the suspenders on his tuxedo stretch with him.

"I get your point," I say. "So how many at this dinner tonight should wear bifocals but won't?"

"Sweet pea, at our age they're just pleased that they are up and about and not slung low." Then he adds, "It's your life wound and your battle medal."

Honey is just like a guy, and he's my guy, straightening his funky glasses frames. "No one will see your purple scar unless they have X-ray vision," he reassures.

But he and I have seen it, and we've run our fingers along the thin scar. It's between us in the silent lines that fan from his eyes and in the deep brackets around his smile and in the strength of his arm as he pulls me to his side.

I shrug my shoulders. He's right. It would shock me and my dinner companions if my neckline plunged that deep, to where my scar is visible. So, it would seem, the only evidence, to the very observant with twenty-twenty vision, is lopsidedness. And that could be just the way I was born to a stranger's gaze or to those who have forgotten the cause. It was a long time ago to those on the periphery of our lives.

My breast scar is on the side that military personnel display medals with pride when they are in dress uniform. When I look at a veteran's dangling medals as he marches proudly on Veteran's Day, I don't know exactly why he received them. I only know that he, or she, was in harm's way and survived.

Some days, though, I don't want to be known as a survivor. I just want to be everyday Jane with a breast-size challenge. I turn and salute myself. I'm marching in my uniform with my wound hidden and my chest uplifted by a support bra.

I was supposed to be the healthy partner on this team. I had a strong gene pool with no known cancer. According to his family history, I would be left behind, financially secure while I moved alone through the remaining milestones of life. The scattering of shadows on the mammogram changed that plan. In the dark, we joked that he could hire a tall blonde housekeeper from my insurance cache instead of me hiring a buff handyman from his.

Initially, we stumbled in stunned disbelief at this twist of fate. Then, in a philanthropic moment while we grappled with the potential diagnosis, we said, "Why not us?" We're baby boomers, the group for which one in eight women are diagnosed with breast cancer; it's our turn. We have a happy marriage, two healthy sons, a large extended family with whom to share holidays, successful careers, a comfortable home, good friends, a growing retirement fund, and plans for European vacations. A breast could be considered a small price for participating in the good life.

Reality set in when I saw my surgeon's eyes between her mask and cap as she positioned the drape circling my left side and as I began counting backward, knowing that this time I would have a breast when I woke up. The agreed-upon procedure was removal of tissue from around the end of the wire biopsy; we would discuss the larger decisions after that.

Fifteen days later, with the wound covered and hidden in my bra, I went about my normal daily routine. While the washing machine churned and spun, I sorted through the mail, smiling at the thoughtfulness of friends. But when I read the last page of the latest church bulletin, my stomach churned and my mind spun with the machine. When you live in a small town, you can't keep any secrets, but what I couldn't decide in my agitated state was whether this was the work of a charitable friend or a busybody. After stuffing the darks into the dryer and the whites into the washer, I picked up the phone receiver, stabbed at the numbers for the church office, and with icicles dripping from my tongue demanded that my name be removed from the prayer circle. "Thank you very much, but I'm not dying."

I still feel badly for that call. I thought I was in control. I was wrong.

Research, learning more about what I was up against, gave me a focus, a semblance of control. I spent hours on the Internet and had in-depth appointments with the surgeon, and finally, we took the leap and made an educated dice toss to choose minimal treatment for grade one, stage one carcinoma. This time when I was counting backward, I knew I'd awake with a pump attached to my armpit, because the surgeon was taking lymph nodes.

Afterward, as I retched into a kidney basin, I also knew that it might not be my last surgery, depending on the lab results from the lymph nodes.

Surrounded by medical staff, I felt safe. I wanted to stay in my hospital bed surrounded by flowers and cards until the results were in, but I was released. Waiting wasn't critical; it could happen at home.

The next day, my sister-in-law drove me back into the city at 25 miles per hour as the wind and snow whipped around the car, because my sutures had broken from their moorings. My breast flesh gaped. The red, raw wound was too much for me to look at. Through hiccupped sobs, while the emergency room doctor closed the gap, I explained to him that I had breast cancer.

While waiting to find out whether additional surgery would be necessary, inching fingertips up beige bedroom walls and squeezing stress balls became my new routines. And I would read the newspaper obituaries with elbows resting on the table, dreading when a woman of my age died and reading the request for funds to go to breast cancer research or to palliative care. I decided that, when my time came, my obituary would say, "Send flowers. I gave in my will."

Those moments when we felt blindsided by the possibility of terminal breast cancer are almost behind us now. All that remains are yearly checkups, my annual survivors' victory lap in the Relay for Life, almost even breasts, and a fuzzy purple scar that blends with blue veins when I examine them without bifocals. When my breasts are tender, believing it is probably normal and the cancer is not back is the middle-age reality upon which we plan our todays and tomorrows.

I turn my back to Honey. "Will you fasten this necklace, please?"

"Sure thing." His breath whispers against the fine hairs on my neck.

"We're good to go."

—Annette M. Bower

Before and After

Inevitably, while sitting in the doctor's office waiting room, thumbing through some beauty magazine, I'll come across a before and after photograph. Sometimes it's an obvious retouch, the before a wrinkled hag, the after a supermodel look-alike. My personal favorite is the borderline obese woman, spilling out of a bikini she has no business wearing, and the after, with hands on trim hips, six-pack abs, big hair, and a smile to match.

Today is my after, but my picture won't look anything like theirs. My pictures won't even show my face. They may end up posted on the Internet, but no one will know it's me, unless I tell them, and at this stage of my life, I just might. Today I'll walk into my plastic surgeon's office, maybe for the last time, and show off his handiwork. But I am not a beauty-obsessed, forty-four-year-old trying to look half my age; mine is not a quest for the elusively perfect physique or wrinkle-free skin.

I am a survivor, and my doctor gave me back what cancer took away: my breasts. And not just any breasts. These are not twisted, lumpy, scarred implants that look like mismatched sisters. These are spectacular, symmetric, perky works of art, prettier than the ones I had before. These are crafted all from me, surgically moved from my tummy to my chest without violating my stomach muscles at all, the miracle of modern reconstruction known as the DIEP surgery. Of course, I'd still give them back for my own droopy, ultrasensitive ones in a minute if I had the choice, because as pretty as my new breasts are, they don't allow me to feel the way I could before. Before, though, is no longer a possibility for me. I'm an after girl now, and happy to be here.

But before . . .

Before, I took life for granted, like most everyone else. I criticized my shape, my hair, my fat belly, and my skinny eyelashes. Before, my husband wasn't measuring up, he worked too hard, played too little, and didn't appreciate me enough. Before, my kids were in trouble too often, left their clothes all over the house, and were often immature and irresponsible. Before, I wanted more, wanted different, wanted a break.

That was Before.

And this is After.

The doctor's office even looks different to me now. On this, my after day, I bounce in full of life and joy. The receptionist comments on how great I look. I take the compliment with grace and smile. Definitely *not* before! I remember all the places I've sat in this room over the last two years: Waiting for my consultation, unsure of everything ahead. Coming in the day before my surgery to be marked up like an engineer's schematic, trying to laugh off my terror. My first checkup, hunched over with seven plastic bulb drains hanging off various parts of my body, wondering what I must have been thinking to do this to myself. The expectation after the nipple reconstruction surgery, when they took the gauze donuts off a week later, and how horrified I was at how mangled they looked; how could I have known then how pretty they would turn out. The day of silly joking when the nipples had healed and they tattooed color on them. Each trip had a different emotional impact.

Today is my after, my glorious conclusion, my picture day. I am dancing in the chair, waiting for the doctor, my feet dangling, swinging like a little girl. I love Dr. Keller; he's a genius, an artist with a spunky personality and a comforting bedside manner. He rescued me from being flat-chested and scarred. He was my champion when I had a complication after surgery and no one believed there was a problem; Dr. Keller had me back in surgery in a flash, kicking assorted butts along the way. He even saved the breast with the bleeder that leaked almost a quart of blood into his new construction zone.

Dr. Keller comes in with his usual smile, and I beam at him.

"How are you?" he asks. He knows enough about me to know that could be a loaded question. But I am so ready for it today.

"Good, good, good!" I answer emphatically.

"Well, it's about time, isn't it? Seems like, for a while there, every bird flying overhead looking for a place to poop was aiming at your head." He sports an impish smile that tells you he may look harmless but is really trouble if you get him going. To me, his presence is huge, but in reality, he is slight, and his smart, pin-striped suit looks almost big on him. We laugh, and he takes a seat on his stool.

"Well, let's see 'em."

And I fling open my robe. Normally, I am not bubbly and immodest, but I figure, he's seen parts of me I've never seen, and I'm proud of his work.

"Wow, they look beautiful! Has Kelly seen these?" he says. Kelly is the new physician's assistant, and we haven't met yet. "Do you mind?" he asks, peering over his glasses, knowing I'd never say no to him.

"Nah, bring her in. I'll flash anybody you want." If he asked me to, I probably would. It's all so non-sexual. As soon as my old breasts came off, these new ones became like a painting Dr. Keller created and lets me carry around. I don't mind showing it off, either; after all, he did a great job.

Kelly is a little shy. While she quietly admires Dr. Keller's handiwork, he and I joke around. For a change, I tell him happy news. I am chatting away with my robe wide open like it's the most natural thing in the world.

"Kelly, get the camera please."

Well, here it comes, my big moment. I can't believe I'm having this much fun. If the doctor did get my face in the picture, I'd be grinning ear to ear. He snaps away, close to a dozen pictures, and I don't stop smiling the whole time.

"Hey, where's the fan blowing my hair?" I laugh.

"Sorry, no music either," he says.

What a change from before. The first time we met, I was on the verge of tears the whole time. I sat with my little note pad, asking questions and looking at my sister-in-law for support. I was so terrified of breast cancer and its treatment that I took the posi-tion of a researcher instead of a patient. I looked at the picture book in disbelief, the same book I'll have my own pictures in very soon. Some petrified woman will look at my before and after and find the courage to go on in the tattooed nipples of a stranger. What a bizarre world we live in, my own piece of it the most bizarre I know.

But this is after, and after is a different world than before. I no longer take life for granted; to me each day is precious, and I know I'm not guaranteed another. I don't make fun of my body, either. I even like the scar that runs from one hip to the other. My fat belly became my beautiful breasts in Dr. Keller's hands, and my skinny lashes are just fine, thank you. I never have a bad hair day, because I love it every day, remembering what it was like to be bald. Ironically, I am more confident and secure in this battered and reconstructed body than I ever was in the body of my youth.

My husband learned to appreciate me, too, even though it took his being ravaged by lymphoma for him to slow down and see what was really important in life. In the end, I was his hero, and we shared a love many healthy people will never know. When I said goodbye to him, I knew that love would follow us into eternity, and I was happy he would be at peace.

How much time did I waste wanting things to be just so, before?

The break I used to want *before* I realize *after* would merely be time away from what I cherish, so I'm not asking for it anymore. Kids' clothes no longer litter my floor, and I would give anything to have my son's white sneakers to trip over and to have one more heart-to-heart talk with him about growing up. But he has already journeyed to the other side, on a crazy motorcycle that took him there just months before my diagnosis and on the very day my husband received his diagnosis. In this *after*, I don't have three sons anymore, but I do have a beautiful granddaughter who looks just like my lost son and has his smile.

After, I am finally happy with what I have. The only thing I want more of is time.

—*Jeanne Schambra*

This story was first published in Mamm *magazine, March/April 2008.*

The Luckiest Family on the Block

Daddy ran his fingers through Mother's short, brown curls as he kissed her goodbye. Her hair had grown back with more gray in it than before the chemotherapy, but she was so glad to be through with wigs and turbans she didn't care.

I watched from the kitchen table as I finished my tuna salad sandwich and potato chips. Daddy came home for lunch nearly every day, even though it was a forty-five-minute drive across town. Since her breast cancer had returned—this time it had metastasized to her lung—it was as though he couldn't get enough of just looking at Mother, making sure she was okay.

"Dr. Durham's office called this morning," she told him. "They said my CAT scan was good, so I can keep taking this chemo. If it had been a bad report, they would've wanted to try something new. 175

But this one seems to be working, so they said I can stick with it."

Daddy clapped his hands together. "That's marvelous!" he said, his blue eyes twinkling. "That's fantastic! We're the luckiest family on the block."

After he got back in the old brown Impala to return to work, Mother sat down and finished her lunch. True Southerners, we both sipped ice tea from tall, blue glasses that matched the blue rooster wallpaper in our kitchen.

The red-brick, 1950s ranch-style house was no mansion—three bedrooms and two small bathrooms—but it was charming. Mother had made all the draperies herself, and everyone who saw them marveled. They looked like they'd been installed by a fancy curtain maker. And she had painted all the rooms and hung the wallpaper herself. She enjoyed staying busy, and no home improvement project daunted her.

Since her cancer had come back, she'd been determined to make the most of all the time she spent sitting in doctors' waiting rooms, and she'd taken up needlepoint. Now, there were dozens of cushions and pictures, lovingly stitched with pictures of flowers, kittens, and other designs that caught Mother's fancy.

The white wall phone rang. I answered, determined that Mother would eat. She'd lost so much weight during her chemo, the last thing she needed was to skip a meal.

"Is Mister Gooch there?" asked a businesslike woman.

"No," I replied.

"Do you know when he'll be back?" she persisted. "This is very important, and I must talk to him before five o'clock."

I recognized the routine and realized the caller was a bill collector.

"Just leave a number," I said, "and I'll have him call you."

"It's most important that I talk to him as soon as possible," the bill collector said. "Are you Missus Gooch?"

"No. I'm their daughter."

"Well, please let me speak to Missus Gooch. It's urgent."

"She can't come to the phone right now."

"This is very important. I really must talk to Mister or Missus Gooch immediately."

I sighed. "Just give me the number. I'll have one of them call you back as soon as I can."

I jotted the number on the notepad on the kitchen counter. After I hung up, I sat back down and tried to eat the last two bites of my sandwich. The toasted bread had grown cold, and it suddenly seemed dry and tasteless.

The bill collector calls had become an unpleasant routine that we tried to ignore. Worrying about money couldn't be good for Mother's recovery.

I picked up the remote control for the little TV. "Let's see if *Family Feud* is on," I said. Neither of us mentioned the phone call. There was nothing we could do about it.

After washing the dishes, I got ready for my job as a copy clerk at the newspaper. I worked there in the evenings and attended classes at the state university in the mornings. I usually wore blue jeans and a T-shirt in the mornings. My habit was to come home for lunch and to slip into some dress slacks and a blouse for work. I made enough money at the newspaper to pay my tuition and car insurance, but I didn't really contribute to the household.

I never told Daddy about the call from the bill collector, and I doubt if Mother did. He knew there were bills that needed to be paid, but there wasn't much he could do.

Mother was improving after her last round of chemo, but she wasn't strong enough to work. She'd had cancer since I was eight years old. And thanks to lots of prayer and good medicine, she had lived to see me grow up and start college.

But her medical care had been expensive. The insurance that Daddy's employer offered had a

$2 million lifetime limit per person. It seemed incredible, but Mother had exceeded the $2 million, and the insurance would no longer pay toward her care. She was sixty years old, too young for Medicare.

So we just tried not to think about the bills and to talk about pleasant things.

"Janie and Luther left on their cruise to Alaska yesterday," Mother said.

Janie and Luther Lester were Mother and Daddy's best friends at church. Once, when Mother was in the hospital, I came home to feed Freckles, our cocker spaniel, and found Luther mowing our front yard. Janie called Mother every day and brought chicken casserole and homemade pound cake.

But in some ways it hurt to see them. Janie was sixty, like Mother, and Luther was sixty-five, like Daddy. But unlike Daddy, Luther had been able to retire. He and Janie enjoyed playing golf and going on trips. We were happy for their good fortune, but it also made us wistful.

Daddy was in his mid-sixties and limping, because he couldn't afford to take time off from work to have the knee surgery the doctor said he needed. He certainly had no hope of retiring, like Luther.

One afternoon when Daddy came home for lunch, he seemed to be moving quicker than usual. He had some papers for Mother to sign. He wanted to take them to the bank before he had to get back to work. The papers would enable them to get money, using their home as collateral. It was called a mortgage. Mother seemed relieved. They would have money to pay the bills and the collection phone calls would end. But, she told me, if they missed payments, the bank would be able to take the house in a foreclosure. It seemed scary.

"It's just not right that you and Daddy have to go through so much," I said.

Daddy laughed. "Don't you worry about us. We're the luckiest family on the block," he said. "The reason we have bills is because your mother has a kind of cancer the doctors can treat. Yeah, we have to pay for it. But consider the alternative: What if she had a kind of cancer they couldn't treat? . . .

"We've been very fortunate."

He was right, of course. Cancer patients whose disease is treatable are very fortunate. But even more important is the ability to recognize the good luck and appreciate it.

Mother and Daddy had many happy years after that, and Daddy never seemed to mind heading to work each day. It was his pleasure to do everything he could to take care of Mother. Eventually he got to have his knee surgery, and we pampered him while he recovered.

Knowing that it meant so much to Daddy for her to stay well, Mother had no choice but to be a good patient and do all she could to stay healthy. She never missed a doctor's appointment and took care of herself by eating spinach, broccoli, and other nutritious foods, even when she might have preferred to skip a meal.

Both of my parents were thankful for the years that the cancer treatment had bought them, and neither even mentioned the financial cost. Their legacy was teaching me to appreciate each day and the good things in my life. Not everyone has the ability to recognize the good things in life, but we did. After all, we were the luckiest family on the block.

—*Beth Gooch*

Staying Afloat

For beachcombers along the Pacific Northwest coast, there is no find more precious than a Japanese fishing float. These small, renegade bubbles of glass, some of which escaped the woven nets of Japanese fishermen more than a hundred years ago, have traveled across thousands of miles of open ocean. They have ridden the crests of tsunamis; they have been buffeted about by typhoons; they have escaped obliteration against the great steel hulls of cargo ships. And, eventually, a few come to rest, battered but intact, on the rocky beaches of Oregon, Washington, and British Columbia.

In the summer of 2003, my husband and I celebrated our twentieth anniversary with a trip to Vancouver Island, a lush, idyllic blend of land and water, a two-hour ferry ride from the cosmopolitan city of Vancouver. Exploring the Canadian island's small towns and coastal villages, we soon discovered how thoroughly the inhabitants have embraced these sturdy, serendipitous gifts of glass that have washed up on their shores. Fishing floats were everywhere, in all sizes and colors, but mostly in endless shades of blue and green, as if they were born of the sea. We saw them lined up along windowsills, nestled in flowerbeds, and piled high in sandy baskets on the weathered front porches of beach houses. Yet, they did not appear to be closely guarded possessions. It was as though the people who had placed them there somehow understood and accepted that this was but another temporary stop in a long and restless journey.

Naturally, I found myself longing to find a fishing float of my own, and this single-minded quest soon had me in full hunter-gatherer mode during our daily explorations of the remote beaches and coves that encircle the island. While I did gather indelible memories of fog-shrouded mornings giving way to brilliant breezy days, of misty evergreen forests pungent with the scent of cedar and pine, of salt spray and gray whales and puffins, I never did come upon a fishing float wedged among a scatter of driftwood or bobbing, jewel-like, in a tide pool. Ultimately, I adopted a philosophical approach to my search, convincing myself to give it up to the universe, to happy chance, that with something like this, there was such a thing as trying too hard.

As it turned out, we spent the last day of our trip on another type of expedition—scouring the abundant local shops for gifts to bring home to family and friends. In particular, I needed to find something special for my mother, because in keeping our two children for ten days she had made this whole trip possible. A well-traveled woman of discriminating tastes for whom T-shirts are decidedly not an option, Mom is not an easy person to buy for. It was one of those times when I had no idea what I was looking for; I only knew I'd know it when I found it. Unfortunately, it was growing late in the day, and I hadn't found it yet. Time was running out when I came across a none-too-promising gallery perched on the second floor of a ramshackle clapboard building above a highly aromatic fishing charter out-fit. Desperate, I climbed the crooked wooden staircase and was amazed to come upon a light-filled room brimming with original art and locally made crafts of every description. And there in the center of the room, suspended from the ceiling by varying lengths of fishing line and sparkling in the dusty sunlight, were a dozen or more fishing floats, girded by the artist with a narrow band of sterling silver and adorned on one side with a delicate silver starfish.

In the end, I bought four. One, of course, was for my feisty, elegant mother, who was once told to give up her "girlish whim" of becoming a doctor but became a fine one, anyway, and who finished raising four children on her own when my father abruptly left after twenty-five years of marriage. One was for my sister and soul mate, who nearly died of a brain tumor in 1999, but whose miraculous recovery and restored health is a constant source of joy and inspiration to everyone who knows her. The third was for a dear friend who had just lost her mother but had somehow retained her infectious buoyancy despite a fickle undertow of grief. The last one was simply an extra, because I knew there would be someone someday who would need such a beautiful talisman of resilience. Little did I know that, less than three months later, that someone would be me.

It was not long after my diagnosis of early-stage breast cancer the following October that I unwrapped the remaining fishing float and hung it in my kitchen window. Facing east, it caught and held the first feeble light of many dark days during that fall and winter. Through two surgeries and eight weeks of radiation, it offered both reminder and proof that I, too, could ride out the storm.

I still hope to find a fishing float "in the wild" someday, but until then, I've made up a story about being the first to find this one and it serves me well.

It is early morning on the far west coast of Vancouver Island. The fog has just lifted, and I sit on a fallen log at that place where the dark, evergreen forest meets the sea. I'm alone on the wide, windswept beach with only the thundering surf and the cry of gulls for company. Shading my eyes with my hand, yet still squinting against the brightness, I scan the horizon, spotting here and there the distant, cloud-like sighs of the gray whales as they pass by on their way to their summer feeding grounds. Eventually, I lower my gaze to the shoreline, to the haphazard piles of driftwood, and to the tidal pools filling with the inrushing tide.

All of a sudden, I see something unexpected amidst a tangle of kelp, and with a gasp of recognition, I leap up and run to the water's edge. I bend down to pick it up, pausing just long enough to rinse it in the waves. Standing in the wet sand, I cradle it with both hands, then laugh at myself for treating it so gently. I can see a tiny hairline crack, can make out the shadowed pattern where the net used to be.

I become aware of my own rapid breathing, of the sound of my pulse in my ears.

I raise my arms, and lifting my treasure toward the racing clouds and climbing light, I marvel at how it has endured.

—Caroline Castle Hicks

Excerpted from Such Stuff as Stars Are Made of: Thoughts on Savoring the Wonders in Everyday Life, *a collection of essays and poems by Caroline Castle Hicks, CPCC Press, 2007.*

Mind Over Cancer

The day I found the lump, I knew. Stephen knew too. I said to him, "Feel this. It wasn't there before, right?" We were watching TV, so humoring me, with half his attention, he let me put his hand to my breast. He pulled back immediately with a look of alarm. I had never seen him lose his composure like that. My rock, my strong, confident, unshakable partner, looked panic-stricken . . . just for a moment, but it was a moment I will never forget. There have been many of those moments this past year. Moments that tested my strength and the strength of my loved ones to a degree that I would not have believed had I not lived it.

Prior to my life-changing discovery, I was under the misguided assumption that after burying both of my parents by the age of twenty-one, life could only

get easier. Little did I know those crises were just a

warm-up for the marathon they call breast cancer. The weeks following my discovery are in some ways a blur, but in others they are too vivid for my liking.

As I drove to the medical center where I was to have a mammogram and ultrasound, I tried to shake the dread I felt inside. I reviewed all the positive choices I'd made with respect to my body over the years and compared them to what I knew contributed to breast cancer. No one in my family had cancer. I was a competitive gymnast as a child and a dancer until the birth of my daughter, and I am a long-time runner who lifts weights and practices yoga and is now a personal trainer. I am a vegetarian, I've never smoked, and I have diligently avoided exposure to toxins. I'd breastfed my daughter for three years, for goodness sake. For twenty-nine years and nine months, my body had been a temple—a stressed-out, Type-A temple, but a temple, nonetheless. This attempt to reassure myself of my low risk for breast cancer should have helped relieve my anxiety. It didn't.

My feelings of dread grew as the technician performed the mammogram and then really intensified when she returned after what seemed like an eternity to take more films. *Is this normal? Does everyone need more views?* I knew the answer was no when, during the ultrasound that followed, that technician made strange faces, muttered to herself, and finally left the room to get the radiologist. By the time she returned with him, I was laying on the table drenched in my own tears, terrified of the direction I instinctively knew my life was taking.

The radiologist told me he was referring me for a biopsy. With a baffled expression, he asked, "Why are you crying?" I couldn't even speak. Did he really have to ask?

I almost drove off the road as I headed home, sobbing until there were no tears left. I cried for my beautiful four-year-old daughter, who would not even remember her mother if I were taken from her now. For Stephen, my soul mate, life partner, and business partner. For our unborn children, who I yearned for but feared I would never have. For my family, who had been through so much already. And for myself. I, too, had been through enough.

I had to wait two agonizing weeks to see the surgeon. Two weeks of going through the motions and of preparing for the holidays with a smile and a pit in my stomach. Two weeks of sleepless nights and tears, of trying to be optimistic but failing miserably.

At the initial appointment with the surgeon, I learned the mammogram showed widespread calcifications that were most likely ductal carcinoma in situ (DCIS) but that the lump I found was probably just a benign cyst. Well, thank God for that lump. If it weren't for that "cute little thing" (the surgeon's words, not mine), I would not have known until it was too late that I needed to have my breast removed before the DCIS mutated and became invasive. It was so widespread and had likely been there for so many years that none of the breast could be saved. I realized fairly quickly that I could deal with the loss of my breast. It was just a breast, after all. I had my life. I had my daughter. And, yippee!—no chemotherapy. . . . Or so I thought.

The appointment with the surgeon was followed by three biopsies: two for the DCIS and one for the lump, just to be sure. I don't think anyone was prepared for the results. That cute little lump turned out to be a highly aggressive invasive cancer that had spread to the nodes under my arm.

I desperately wanted more children, and I wanted to breastfeed those children. I sat in the surgeon's office begging her to tell me I didn't have to give up my dream, only to be told that I needed to stop worrying about having more children and to start being "concerned with living for the next five years." So now I was dying? How did this happen?

I quickly became educated about invasive breast cancer in young women. To my chagrin, I learned this is one instance in which youth is not your friend. In fact, the younger you are, the more aggressive the cancer tends to be. I learned that the type of tumor I had was not sensitive to hormones, which meant I potentially could have more children. However, my celebration was short-lived, as the surgeon went on to explain that this made the cancer was more difficult to treat. I left the office feeling completely dejected and defeated.

Stephen was amazing through the whole ordeal. He gave me exactly a week to mope and feel sorry for myself, which I did with gusto. Once my week was up, he delivered the first of many pep talks. From that point on, we would approach this with nothing less than optimism. We were going to beat this, no matter what. Let the battle begin!

The first thing I did was to find another surgeon, someone who was more kind, upbeat, and empathetic and who saw me, the person, and not just a cancer patient.

Next, I changed my own attitude. I would fight this disease with all that I had. I would fight for my daughter, I would fight for myself, and I would fight for all who cared for me.

The fear, though, still haunted me. It hit me at the strangest times, and I would be overcome with emotion—with grief, anger, and sheer terror of the unknown. I was afraid of so many things: that I would feel unbearably sick and weak; that I, the eternal caregiver, would need someone to care for me; that I might not live to see my daughter grow up.

So I started making a concerted effort to stay positive. I began to live in faith and with strength instead of in fear and with dread. Every day, several times a day, I repeated to myself, "I am strong, I am healthy, and I have energy." I visualized my body without cancer. Day and night, I practiced being optimistic. I tried to speak only positive words. Even during the most difficult moments of chemotherapy, I went to work, smiled, and told anyone who asked (and everyone did) that I "felt great" with as much sincerity as I could muster. And you know what? It worked. I began feeling better physically and mentally. This new reality carried me through.

Another attitude-changing strategy was refusing to allow cancer to consume and control my life. During the twenty weeks of chemo, I kept my schedule as close to normal as possible. I drove myself to treatments, because it made me feel in charge. I worked, exercised, and enjoyed my life. I put on my head scarves and went out. I made love—beautiful, passionate, amazing love. I helped at my daughter's school, hosted play dates, baked cookies, laughed, and planned our future.

Finally, I changed my mind-set about accepting help from others and adopted an "attitude of gratitude." Many wonderful people—from close friends to complete strangers—made the year of diagnosis and treatment much more manageable. People I had never met but who knew of my situation through mutual friends offered me complementary spa treatments, helped raise funds for my medical expenses, sent thoughtful gifts and encouraging e-mails, and more. A group of my clients chipped in for a housekeeper to clean my house for months. What a relief it was not to worry about finding the energy to clean. My daughter (with a little help) bought us matching baseball caps and beach hats that I will cherish forever. A friend who is a professional photographer took rolls of film of my daughter and me doing the things we love together. I could go on and on. The outpouring of support was moving and encouraging. I felt engulfed by love.

After the first of sixteen chemo treatments, there was no detectable change in the size of the tumor. But when I changed my mental focus, my body responded. The look on my oncologist's face when she could not find the 3.5 centimeter lump that had been in my breast just two weeks prior was priceless. I had decided to have chemotherapy before surgery, and when the breast was removed, not a single cell of invasive cancer was found in the breast or lymph nodes. I went from having a stage two-B diagnosis and a fairly poor prognosis to an almost stage zero diagnosis with a very promising prognosis. I call that a miracle. And I truly believe it had everything to do with my new attitude.

As a personal trainer who has seen the benefits of remaining active and fit during treatment, I know firsthand the importance of gaining and maintaining strength both during and after treatment. So I now help women with breast cancer to stay fit and active during and after treatment and surgery. It is so rewarding to hear how much better they feel after a workout and to see the smiles on their faces when I tell them how well they are doing. I hope to continue this work on a larger scale after I complete my treatments. Having breast cancer has strengthened my passion for and my commitment to my work—helping people to become strong in body, spirit, and mind. It's what I was born to do.

Having breast cancer also enabled me to overcome many fears. I faced the big C and won. I beat cancer. I cheated death. And I will go on to have babies and to breastfeed (on one side, but nonetheless). But the greatest victory for me has come from within, from the changes in my heart and mind. I will never again look at life in the same way. Now, I value every moment, every experience, and every challenge. I'm filled with hope and peace and gratitude . . . and love.

—*Kate Kenworthy*

The Pebble and the Rock:
A Love Story

I remember distinctly what an especially beautiful July day it was. The warm sun against the cool blue ocean and the park filled with lush foliage and tropical flowers was picture-perfect as we strolled along the garden path. My husband and I often remark how lucky we are to live in Laguna Beach. "Pinch me. Tell me it's real," we joke. That's how beautiful it is here.

But the beauty and warmth of the day could not keep away the coldness I felt inside. I stared at the boats on the horizon. Where was my ship? Where was I headed?

I picked up a pebble as we walked along the beach. "Look, honey. A pebble. I'm a pebble."

"Stop it," my husband insisted. "You're no pebble."

"Yes, I am."

I felt so small, wishing I could wash away to sea. My head was swimming. I couldn't believe the news I'd heard today. After fourteen years of being cancer-free, the demon had come back.

Alan reached down and grabbed a bigger rock and placed it in my palm along with the little pebble. "See, you've become much bigger in no time."

I smiled for about half a second. Then both of our eyes welled as his hand clenched mine, holding the rock and pebble. "You beat it before, you know."

I nodded but wanted to hear no more, and Alan sensed that. "Take me home," I said. It's hard to describe—I wanted to be with him, but I also wanted to be alone. I wanted to cry. By myself. I wanted to think about my mom.

Thirty years ago, my mother died of breast cancer. I was in my twenties with my whole life ahead of me. I witnessed a vibrant, outgoing giant of a woman shrivel into a helpless stick figure. It was the saddest time of my life. As she lay in her hospital bed doped up with drugs, I remember her doctor saying, "I hope your mother passes away this weekend. She has suffered enough."

I pictured her pretty face and imagined mine. The genes that had made my mother so beautiful were passed on to me, as was the predisposition for breast cancer. How could we be so blessed and so cursed at the same time?

I could not believe I had cancer again! I looked and felt great—a woman in her fifties who still looked and felt forty. Just a few weeks earlier, a kid in town had wolf-whistled at me and yelled, "Hi, Goldie Hawn!" I got such a kick out of that. Now, my looks and everything I enjoyed about myself would be held hostage by the monster. What kind of evil could ravage its victims without them even knowing it, when they looked and felt their best?

When I was diagnosed the first time, I'd been terrified, but the fear I felt with the recurrence was even stronger. In 1991, I'd felt a small lump in my left breast—which I didn't ignore, even though I'd had a "clear" mammogram just a few months before. As it turned out, I had stage one invasive breast cancer. I felt very lucky, because I caught it early and needed only a lumpectomy and radiation and no "adjuvant" therapy (chemo or hormonal). I was given a great prognosis, and after about seven years, my oncologist didn't even want to see me anymore, proclaiming me "cured."

But I wasn't cured. On July 8, 2005, my worst fear was confirmed.

The first hint of trouble had come out of the blue, wholly unexpected, while I was eagerly anticipating a trip to my hometown of Minneapolis for my niece's wedding. I would be seeing friends and family I hadn't seen in a while. I was so excited. Then, a few weeks before the wedding, I noticed a tiny red blemish near my left breast. At first, I thought it was just a mole and called my skin doctor to check it out. The earliest appointment was the morning after I would return from the wedding, on July 5. I went to the wedding and had a great time, but on the flight home the upcoming appointment gnawed at me.

After examining me, the doctor asked when I'd last had a mammogram. It wasn't that long ago and had been clear. What could this "skin thing" have to do with that? She ordered an immediate mammogram. Why couldn't it wait? I had one scheduled in a month. It made no sense; still, it was scaring the life out of me. I knew I would have to stay calm and not let on to Alan, who I was sure would fall apart.

I had the mammogram the next day and waited in the waiting room for the results. Looking at the technician, I knew. He didn't have to say a word. "We need to do a biopsy," he said. It was like being hit by a train. Now I had to tell Alan. As I predicted, he fell apart. He, too, had lost his mother, to non-Hodgkins cancer, when he was just twenty-one.

I had a needle biopsy, and Alan made an appointment with my original breast cancer surgeon the following day. Seeing Dr. West after all those years made me cry. He'd saved my life fourteen years earlier; could he save me again? Dr. West walked in and gave me a big hug. He was comforting, but he didn't have good news. It was likely cancer; I was likely going to have a mastectomy and reconstruction. What did he mean by "likely?" Did he mean I might spare my breasts like the last time? What was my prognosis? So many questions were fighting for attention. He assured me I wouldn't have to make all the decisions "right away," because they didn't know everything "yet"—but as I have learned about breast cancer, "not right away" often means days. With cancer, one has to become an expert in the disease in a short time. Making the wrong decision can be life-altering, if not life-threatening.

Looking back, I think my biggest fear was the dreaded chemo—the horrible effects, among them losing my hair and, with it, my looks and identity. Could that be avoided? "Probably not," was the unfortunate reply. The question was whether I was a candidate for pre-op chemotherapy. Some choice: not a question of whether I'd need chemo, but when— before or after surgery. As it turned out, the tumor was stage three, grade B. The "skin involvement" was no coincidence; the lesion itself was cancerous.

I decided to have a bilateral mastectomy to prevent any further problems as well as a transflap procedure, whereby new breasts would be constructed of skin removed from my back. I was convinced I would be a freak for life. In a matter of days, my beautiful body, which I had spent years working on, spending a fortune on gyms, spas, you name it, would be gone— just like that. And if I didn't end up a freak, I certainly would not be a "real" woman anymore. Would my husband still love me? Would I still love me?

After surgery, I would have to decide on chemo.

"What if I don't do this?" I asked one of the oncologists. "What would be the outcome?"

The answer was simple: there would be no outcome. That was all I needed to hear. I would do whatever it took, whatever the cost. I resigned myself that, even if I lost my hair and figure, I wouldn't lose my love of life.

With the diagnosis confirmed and treatment plans in place—surgery end of July, followed by chemo from September 15 through December 30—Alan and I again went to the beach to walk and talk and reflect on this difficult time. I felt the rock and the pebble from our previous walk weeks before bouncing around in my sweatshirt pocket. That's how I felt the week before surgery as I bounced between Dr. West, my oncologist, the great Dr. Neil Barth, chief of staff at Hoag Hospital, and my brilliant plastic surgeon, Dr. Ivan Turpin, and again for six months afterward as I sought second opinions regarding the safety and necessity of radiation treatment from doctors on both the East and West Coasts.

When it was time to leave our home to go to the hospital, I cried and hugged Alan. By then, he had regrouped and become my take-charge supporter. He was amazing, getting everything I needed, calling doctors, obtaining my old records, you name it. So, naturally, when I reminded him to bring my rock for my surgery, he told me not to worry. He put his hand in his pocket and pulled it out. I smiled and looked at him, "That's not what I was referring to, dummy."

He looked at me, puzzled. "What do you mean?"

"My real rock—you."

My rock stands six feet tall, has wonderful dark wavy hair (which I envied every day I went through chemotherapy), and is teddy bear size for great hugs. He has a heart of gold and is unselfish in every way. My rock is the guy who made appointments, put his business on hold, and flew across the country for second opinions. Who is on the Internet checking out every medical article on breast cancer. Who asks every doctor every question imaginable. That is my rock. The rock in my life.

Through the slow and painful post-op recovery and through the grueling chemotherapy, I always kept a positive attitude. Yes, despite losing my hair. Even on my weakest days, when I couldn't get out of bed, I knew I'd get back on my feet. After all, I had my rock, along with many wonderful friends and strangers who helped me through this difficult time. My support team—which included the Susan G. Komen organization and my boss, who kept my job open for me for a long while—was there for me financially and spiritually.

Now, two years later, I count my blessings every day. Although I still fear recurrence, I feel fortunate and am confident the future holds even more promise for my daughter and granddaughter, should they be faced with breast cancer one day. I have incredible doctors who look after me. Currently cancer-free, I feel good and look good again, too. One would never know I had surgery, and my hair is back—and in style! I've even had time to work on my art, which eased the pain of recovery. Before breast cancer, I had taken painting and various art classes over the years but never had much time to work on my style. Throughout my recovery period, I had a chance to really explore my artistic side, which includes painting and creating fabric purses. Today, I am a featured artist at the Sawdust Art Festival in Laguna Beach.

I no longer feel like a small, inconsequential pebble about to be washed away into the ocean. I now know that a pebble, though small, is as strong and substantial as any mountain. So, like the pebble, I go in and out with the tide, flowing with the ebbs of fate, grateful to be alive and well. Most of all, though, I am thankful for my husband. My rock.

—*Rosalie Marsh-Boinus*

Saving Grace

Everyone always tells you that it is important to keep your sense of humor. Of course, this sage advice usually comes from someone who is the epitome of good health, but it can also come from those who have been there. I've been there, and believe me, humor has often been my saving grace.

In August 2005, I had a right modified mastectomy following a diagnosis of stage zero ductal carcinoma in situ (DCIS) and a lumpectomy where clear margins could not be obtained.

Shortly after that, I received my temporary breast form in the mail from the American Cancer Society. It looked more like a stuffed egg than a breast, and it came with instructions how to make it look like you wanted by adding or taking away the stuffing. Because it really had no weight to it, like a breast does, the brochure advised the wearer to add weights to it. It recommended fishing weights, metal washers, and the like. There was no information as to how much a particular size and cup weighed. I had never thought about the weight of a breast (except in the summer when everything was too hot and too heavy). I still had one breast left, but can you really weigh that? I did put my breast on the bathroom scale, but it didn't register as anything. I even tried my food scale, but that didn't work either. I'm glad my family didn't see me doing that. They would never have looked at the food scale the same way again.

I searched the house for what to put in the form as weights. Hmmm. No fishermen in the house, so no fishing weights. Nuts and bolts were too oddly shaped. Batteries? Too heavy, and what would happen when I had a hot flash? I envisioned my body sweating and jerking at the same time—not a pretty picture. Washers? Perfect! They were even circular, like breasts relatively are. A good match. I grabbed a small handful of washers from my husband's workshop and added them to the form. I mooshed them around until I thought it filled my usual C cup, pinned up the back of my egg/breast, and felt pretty secure. I was ready to finally go out in public.

When I ran up the basement steps from the workshop, two of the washers found their way out the back of my form and rolled down the inside of my shirt and down the stairs. Oops. My first reaction was, *Thank goodness I was still at home.* How embarrassing that would have been at the grocery store! I envisioned myself chasing rolling washers down the produce aisle and imagined asking for help. "Um . . . my washers fell out of my breast form; can you help me find them?" I could just see the look on their faces as they handed me the washers and watched me do a few gyrations in the aisle trying to secure them where they belonged.

While I wore my form, I continued to try to figure out how much weight to put in it to make it stay where it was supposed to. The darned thing had a habit of creeping up. Sometimes I felt akin to the Hunchback of Notre Dame, except that my hump was in front. Before I would get out of the car, I often turned to my mate and asked if I was even. When he was not available, I asked my teenaged children. They were mortified. They would give me a fleeting sideways glance, quickly look away, and declare, "Mom! You're fine. Don't ask me that again." They were especially grateful when I was finally fitted with a prosthesis.

We lived in Atlanta, Georgia, and around that time, we went to the new Atlanta Aquarium. We had to buy tickets with a specific time on them for admission, because of the big crowds wanting to see the world's biggest aquarium, but we still had to wait in line. As we finally made our approach to what we thought was the entrance, we spied the metal detector that everyone was going through. Uh-oh. Many people were setting it off. I glanced down at my chest. I shot my husband a horrified look. What was I going to do? Should I say something first or wait until the alarm went off? What would I say then? I was sweating like a thief caught red-handed. I could see it now: off to the pokey for me and my form. Or maybe they would make me leave it right there at the admission gates.

I did what I always do in tense situations: I said a breath prayer—you know, one of those quick prayers you say in one breath. I asked God to tell me what to say: *Please put some words into my empty head and help them to come out of my mouth the right way.*

Finally, it was my turn to go through the metal detector, and sure enough, the alarm went off! I waited in line with four or five other people who had set it off too, and I watched as money, belt buckles, cell phones, and the like were put in containers. A young man of eighteen or so was in charge of waving the metal-detecting wand over each person, and if they still beeped, an explanation was requested. This guy could have been Opie Taylor on *Mayberry RFD*—freckle-faced, blue eyes, red hair, and a peach-fuzzed face.

I stepped forward to accept the wand. It beeped at my hip pocket. My cell phone! Because I had worried so much about my washers, I had forgotten about it. Whew! I thought I was off the hook, smiled, and relaxed. The wand beeped again, this time at my breast. The young man frowned slightly, waved it by my breast again, and looked at me quizzically. I took a breath, forced a smile, and said, "I am a breast cancer survivor, and I am wearing a prosthesis." That wasn't as hard to say as I thought it would be.

The young man looked at me for a second or two and turned the most radiant shade of fire engine red. He quickly averted his eyes, stammered something, shuffled his feet like a little boy caught passing a note in class, and waved me on ahead with his wand-less hand. He was more embarrassed than I was. After rejoining my family, my husband and I had a good laugh over it.

I was finally fitted for my prosthesis six months after my mastectomy. Maybe that's where I should have called when I was trying to figure out how much my form should have weighed. Hindsight is a great thing, isn't it? At the time, I didn't even know such places existed. Anyway, I walked into the store feeling a little uncomfortable and told them I was there for a fitting. When I felt the woman's eyes instantly go to my chest, I knew this was going to be a weird experience but that there was sure to be some humor in it somewhere. She led me through the curtain to the fitting area and told the other woman stocking the shelves that she needed some triangles. Triangles? Breasts can be triangles? She measured me up, down, across, and diagonally, and then she left me "draped" in the room. She returned momentarily with six or seven boxes. I watched her manhandle a breast form into the bra. It was like watching a mammogram gone bad.

She helped me put on the bra, and then grabbed the drape from behind and cinched it up against me. "What do you think?"

Spying my pudgy body outlined in green cloth, I smiled inside. "Lay me down, and I could be an advertisement for the rolling hills of Ireland," I said.

She smiled, too, and said, "But I meant, how does the *bra* look and feel?"

The sucker was really tight, and she had given me the tale about how most women wear the wrong size bra and that the support really needs to be in the band, yada yada yada. Did I really need this? I felt like a queen-sized woman trying to convince herself that she could wear size A pantyhose. Grease me up, and I was sure I could do it. How could I decide between a medieval torture device and the hyperactive stuffed breast/egg? In the end, I opted for the constrictor and hoped that my washing machine would wear down those iron-like bands like it did the elastic in my underwear.

Fourteen months after my initial surgery, I am at a point in my life where I am ready to do some reconstruction. When I searched for that term on the Internet, I received thousands of hits for construction companies that specialize in refurbishing antique homes. While I was doing some refurbishing, I certainly was not an antique. I hoped to be one some day, but not now.

I knew I had found the right plastic surgeon when, after examining me and determining a free tram procedure would be best, he said in a deadpan voice, "Now, I'm going to tell you something that no other doctor will tell you." He paused and added, "Don't go on a diet." Yes!

My surgery is set for early December, and I am so excited! I am going to get a new breast and a tummy tuck for Christmas! What woman my age wouldn't be thrilled about that? Plus, the insurance is paying for it. Isn't there a children's Christmas song that goes something like, "All I want for Christmas is my two front . . . somethings?" I think I'll do that in needlepoint.

—Paula Sword

There's No Place Like Normal

I snapped my cell phone shut and dropped it into my purse, and waited for my kid sister to meet me. Although it would take her only five minutes to walk from her office in the hospital to where I was, I paced, impatient that she was not already here. Five short months earlier, I'd been diagnosed with breast cancer. The time between then and now had flown by like a whirling dervish, as though Dorothy's tornado had picked me up in April and whisked me to September in the blink of an eye. But I wasn't in Oz, and I certainly wasn't in Kansas. I was standing at the end of a long carpeted hall with paintings lining the walls outside a massive oak door that hid a roomful of secrets, waiting for Susan to join me.

In a way, everything up to that point had felt surreal. I remember thinking, I don't have cancer. I couldn't have cancer. Cancer was something that happened to someone else. Someone who did not take care of herself. Someone who had a family history of it. Not to me. I exercised. I ate all the right things. I didn't smoke. I came from healthy stock, no family history of breast cancer. I was "normal."

Yet, here I stood.

Susan rounded the corner and joined me. "Can't get in without this," she said, pulling a key out of her pants pocket. "Ready?"

I smiled and nodded, glancing one more time at a gold plaque hanging on the wall next to the door. Its smooth scripted letters read "Wig Room."

Inserting the key into the lock, Susan twisted the brass knob and swung open the door. Although we knew what awaited us, we still gaped in surprise as we stepped into the room, its plush carpet deafening the sounds of our footsteps. Dozens of wigs, all styles and colors, all donated by former cancer fighters, lined shelves and tabletops, waiting to be of service. I paused for a second, overwhelmed. Did I really belong here? Would I actually lose my hair?

Putting her arm around my shoulders, Susan directed me to a chair and seated me in front of a large mirror framed by soft, round light bulbs. For a moment, I felt like a movie star. Behind me, Susan fingered the wigs, trying to decide which one I should try first. Selecting a brown one with a pixie style, she stretched it over my head, stuffing my shoulder-length hair under it.

Studying myself in the mirror from all angles, I nodded, "Not bad. Let's try another."

For the next hour, both of us tried and retried nearly every wig in that room. We laughed and joked, flirting with our bad, sexy selves in the mirror, enjoying how our appearances changed with the different styles and colors. I suppose I laughed a little too loudly at times, because at one point Susan gave me a serious look.

"It's going to be alright," she promised. "We'll get through this together."

Finally, I decided on two short wigs, one brown and the other "dirty" blonde. Initially, I was going to take only one, but Susan assured me I looked natural in each of the two wigs and should borrow both. If I had to lose my hair, I might as well take advantage of being a different woman every other day.

Signing for the two wigs, promising on paper to return them to this library of hair, I placed them in a bag and went home, excited. When my hair did begin to fall, I would have these backups to make me look and feel normal.

It did not take long before my hair submitted to the chemotherapy medications. Every morning and every evening, my hairbrush pulled out hundreds of strands. Sometimes the hair just fell to the floor without any help.

After a couple of weeks, I faced the fact that I had very little hair left. At that point, I retrieved the borrowed wigs from my bedroom closet and decided to wear the brown one first. Adjusting it over my scalp and tucking in the remaining strands of my real hair, I studied myself in the mirror, satisfied. After applying my makeup, I took one more look at myself and nodded. *Yes*, I thought, *I look normal. No one will ever know.*

That evening, when I returned home from work, I yanked the wig from my head and took a long look at it. My first day out in my wig, and all I'd done was wonder incessantly whether everyone could tell it wasn't my real hair. I felt miserable. The pile of synthetic fibers had looked real enough this morning.

"Why does it look fake now?"

I must have asked that question out loud, because a young, soft voice from behind answered. "It's pretty, Mom, but it's not you."

Of course, it was me. I had dark brown hair all of my life. It was as much a part of me as my dimples and green eyes.

Turning around, I met the brown eyes of my four-teen-year-old daughter. "What do you mean, Kel?"

With the blunt honesty that can come only from a teenager, she answered, "You've never been one to hide behind anything, Mom. For you, wearing a wig is not normal."

Stunned, I realized she was right. I turned back to the mirror and looked at my face and my balding head. I stared at the creases that lined the corners of my eyes. I felt the smoothness of my cheeks as I passed my hands over them.

My daughter, somehow understanding a woman's vanity and my concerns, added, "Your smile is your best feature."

Needless to say, I never wore that wig again. Thanks to my daughter's wisdom, I realized that just being me is the most natural—and normal—thing in the world.

—*Jennifer D. Jenkins*

Surviving Period

At thirteen, a horrible thing happened: I started my period. Doubled over with menstrual cramps, I cried, I wailed, and I lamented life, convinced I was being punished for something. I told my mother that the minute I got married I was going to get pregnant and stay that way as much as possible so that I could repeatedly avoid having my period, sneakily skirting nature's system. I was thirteen and obviously an idiot. All I knew was that I was embarking on a new world that involved sitting on bulky pads or experimenting with the terrifying prospect of tampons, and at the crux of the issue was the fact that I was becoming a woman and I wasn't so sure I was ready for the whole thing.

Meanwhile, my mom's best friend was dying. At least, in my small view of the world, this was what I thought was happening to her. Bonnie had lost her hair, and her husband had left her. She'd been sick for about two years, and although we weren't allowed to talk about it in front of her, she'd had a mastectomy. I always eyed her suspiciously when she was over, but I couldn't tell. Her breasts never looked lopsided in sweaters, and being precocious, I'd checked when I thought I couldn't be detected. I wasn't sure whether having one breast or none was why her husband had left, and it seemed indecent to ask. I spent a lot of that year watching her sweaters, focusing on them—maybe because I spent a lot of that year focusing on my own sweaters, too, trying to figure out how to squish them back down as my own breasts were bursting forth.

Bonnie had two sons, the same ages as my younger sister and me. We stopped playing with them right around the time she got sick. I don't really know if her illness had anything to do with that, or if it just coincided with the fact that we had just reached the age when girls stopped playing with boys. We were at that inelegant stage in which, if you were near a boy, you either kissed him or you sort of hated him. Since I had no interest in kissing a boy that I'd repeatedly seen naked since I was two, I stopped playing with the boy my age. I had never stopped to consider the younger one, even when my mom would shake her head after she'd hung up the phone after speaking with Bonnie, sighing and saying, "Thank God for those boys." I'd seen the younger one at the grocery store one day, loading bread and milk into the basket of his bike, and I was still miffed that my mother wouldn't even entertain the argument I'd wanted to have with her about why he was only nine and allowed to ride his bicycle to the store alone and I was thirteen and not allowed to do the same.

The first Christmas Bonnie was sick, what concerned me the most was that we wouldn't be going to her house for our usual Christmas Eve celebration. But, as per usual, we did. No matter how many sneaky glances I stole, I couldn't really tell she was sick. As I sat on the floor of her living room playing video games with her sons, all the hushed tones and head-shaking my mom used when she talked about Bonnie after visiting seemed misplaced. No one even pretended that her terrible appetizers were delicious. While I watched Bonnie flit from guest to guest, the picture of happiness and health, enjoying her family and friends, beaming with joy at the love around her, I felt cheated of all the hours my mom spent with Bonnie instead of with us.

After about the requisite five days, my first period ended. It was over, and I was ready and almost able to forget it had ever happened. I started to move on with my life, pretending I was still a girl, that I didn't have to grow up yet. Then a phone call came that I will never forget. My mother answered, and I only heard her end of the conversation.

"Hello?" She paused, listening to the response. "Oh, my God! That's wonderful! When?" Another pause and then, "Do you think it means you could, well, not that you would, of course…but who cares! I'm so excited for you!" She paused again, longer this time. "Yes, yes, of course. Call me later, after you've called everyone else. We'll talk more. Bye."

After my mom hung up, she came rushing out to the front porch, where I'd been sitting, sunning myself and painting my toenails. She was flapping her hands in excitement, and her cheeks were flushed.

"Oh, Rachel! You won't believe it!" she screamed.

"What?" I was almost as excited as she was now, so infectious was her absolute joy.

"It's Bonnie! She's started her period!"

My jaw dropped. "What?" I asked, stunned.

"She started her period. The chemo and all the medication put her through menopause early, and they told her she'd probably never have one ever again, but she started her period today. Isn't that wonderful?" My mom was truly excited.

"Sure, I guess so?" I said, genuinely questioning my mom's sanity. I stood up and walked on my heels into the house, careful not to damage my toenail polish.

I can't say that I didn't ruminate on this news for at least a little while that afternoon. Although I was a teenager and therefore inherently self-centered, I did find myself intrigued by the idea that this was somehow universally important. At the time, I chalked it up to girl stuff that I didn't understand yet, but deep down I knew it was more than that.

It wasn't until I was almost thirty and had my first child that I understood the joy she'd found. She'd been robbed of so much by her disease, but fate or nature or something had brought back a small part of herself, of her womanhood. At thirteen, I could not understand that. Even now, when I am lying on the couch with cramps and a heating pad, I have to remind myself not to lament my lot in life too often, lest it be taken from me too soon by something I cannot control.

—*Rachel Beth McClain*

The Challenge

How could this be happening to me, the one who never gets sick? Haven't I always followed the health rules: plenty of fruits and vegetables, supplemented with vitamins and minerals, especially vitamin C? I exercise regularly and always enjoy a positive outlook on life. There's no cancer in my long-lived and healthy family history. They must have made a mistake.

Those were my thoughts as my husband, Dean, and I sat in the surgeon's office watching the X-ray of my first mammogram on the lit screen.

The surgeon pointed out the suspicious lump. "Notice the leg-like protrusions. Resembles a crab. That's why they call it cancer."

Great. This sharp-eyed guy, who found a crab in that jumble of tissue, made the diagnosis without even drawing blood. Obviously, he'd made a mistake.

A few weeks before the devastating diagnosis, my daughter-in-law had advised me that her mother's breast cancer had been discovered with a mammogram and that I should get that put-off-for-years breast exam ASAP. Waste of time, I figured, but Debby insisted. So I made the appointment. Her persistent nagging saved my life. Now, as is the custom in some cultures, she'll have to take care of me in my old age. And I want the room with the view!

Since this was my first experience with a mammogram, the technician searching for a radiologist meant nothing to me. While she ran through the halls like a crazy person, I calmly read a pamphlet on the seven signs of impending breast cancer and checked off every one as a definite negative. Just as I finished, the technician showed up with the radiologist she'd dragged from his lab. Despite his serious behavior, I still didn't panic, because all he said was to make an appointment with my family physician, who would explain the X-ray to me.

Dean had remained at work when I went for the initial mammogram. When I returned to the office, I told him that something suspicious showed up in the mammogram but that I was such a low risk for cancer, everything would turn out fine, and he agreed. He accompanied me to every examination and appointment afterward.

The early optimism was sorely tested when we got to our primary care provider. Our straight-from-central-casting doctor was out sick. In the jammed office, we waited more than two hours to see the substitute doctor. Waiting of any kind is not in Dean's nature. This time he couldn't walk out. Annoying or not, we had to learn the truth about the questionable test.

When the doctor finally saw us, we soon found he didn't share our physician's wonderful bedside manner. He blurted out that the tumor was "impalpable," not revealed with a digital breast examination. Though very small, the growth looked suspiciously like breast cancer. He recommended seeing a surgeon immediately. I had to lean on the reception window, stunned, while his nurse made the appointment. Dean kept insisting we'd find all this aggravation would end in a misdiagnosis.

Days later, we sat in the surgeon's office. Neither of us agreed with the surgeon's flash conclusion and nodded our approval when he said the next step would be a biopsy. They scheduled me for a month later. I didn't tell anyone about the pending biopsy and didn't worry much, since I'd convinced myself the results would be negative.

The biopsy procedure, which I'd always thought consisted of a needle into the breast, developed into a full-fledged operation with the surgeon removing the tumor. Although scheduled for the first appointment in the morning, I lay in the hall for more than three hours while all operating rooms opened for victims of a disastrous accident on the interstate. My impatient spouse had to stay in the waiting room outside, leaving me free to plan the rest of my life with the gift of unused time handed to me. I would phase out my radio career and turn back to writing, my first love, and as soon as I got up from this blasted gurney, I'd shop for a computer.

I put together my acceptance speech for winning the Pulitzer as they wheeled me into the operating room. Soon after counting backward while the general anesthetic took over, I was in a room recovering from the ordeal. Dean grouched about the long wait as we eagerly anticipated the surgeon's admission that he'd slipped up in his rush analysis of the crablike tumor. Unfortunately, and unbelievably, we were wrong. The diagnosis backed by lab tests was positive for breast cancer.

The first question I asked the surgeon was, "Suppose I did nothing. What then?"

"You'll die of breast cancer," he said.

Overcoming his shock, Dean had to make a wisecrack. The drains in the incision needed to be changed in the morning, and he volunteered to do it so we wouldn't have to make the trek back to the hospital complex. "I know all about changing drains," my husband said. "We do it all the time for the cows."

The doctor looked at me and said, "Don't you go milking cows."

Despite the gravity of the situation, I couldn't help answering, "Would you put that in writing and add the word 'never.'"

Once I accepted the verdict as fact, even though angst ran rampant through my mind and body, I couldn't help feeling I had an angel on my shoulder directing me to that first mammogram. How blessed that the tumor discovery came while still miniscule, surely resulting in an assured recovery.

Next on the schedule, we had to decide which steps to take to avoid the death sentence the surgeon had pronounced if I did nothing. The cancer team gave me the choice of settling for the lumpectomy, but the surgeon advised against that treatment. So did the oncologist, a real sweetie, with whom I later consulted. The tumor, while small, stood smack up against the chest wall. The X-ray showed a virulent form of cancer, not yet invasive, but surely to become so. Quite a bit of radiation and maybe chemo would follow. As the sweet oncologist said, "You surely have to be in love with your breast to undergo all that."

With a mastectomy, all I had to do afterward was take the hormone pills and see the reconstructive surgeon. I'd never been particularly happy with my bustline, so after looking at all the alternatives, I chose the major surgery. Importantly, my husband heartily agreed. Some women have criticized me for my decision, but now cancer-free, I've never regretted it.

Before the surgery, Dean and I conferred with the plastic surgeon. He explained he would place an expander in the chest wall after the surgeon removed the breast, and about three months later he would insert a silicone prosthesis. Sounded good to me, and I was ready when the day of the operation arrived. The ordeal took five hours, pretty well knocking me out, but by the second day, I felt more like my perky self.

After I'd broken the news to friends and family, they all asked what they could do. I delivered a stock answer to everyone: "Indulge me." In the hospital room after the surgery, decadent extravagances surrounded me. Flowers and candy, of course, books and enough body oils and bath goodies to start my own spa filled all available space. While mourning the loss of a body part, I thoroughly enjoyed the attention and gifts.

Everyone in the hospital treated me like a queen. The solicitous nurses offered anything I wanted to ease the pain, which wasn't much. So my head was clear when a physical therapist stopped by and gave me a rod with instructions to exercise my afflicted left arm where the lymph nodes had been removed. The therapist told me to lift the stick over my head, as high as possible, and slowly bring it down. She emphasized the workout should be repeated often to strengthen that left arm and to ward off debility.

I chose to do the exercise in the patient's lounge near my room. Used by smokers, even those suffering cancer, patients and visitors would gather there to chat and exchange vital information. Some of the stories were quite sad. A young man diagnosed with pancreatic cancer spoke with his wife about ways to tell their children. An older woman, who seemed the fun-loving type, tearfully chain-smoked while waiting for diagnostic tests to determine the cause of a growth on her kidney. Groups of patients sat around the room, conferring tensely with relatives. The somber atmosphere even affected me, as I realized my arm had come out of the surgery quite weakened. I could only get that pesky rod to my shoulder.

Then Dean arrived. Not exactly a by-the-book romantic, he took one look at what I was doing and called out, "Raise that stick over your head when you're ready for sex."

Everyone in the room joined me in laughing at his remark. Forgetting their problems, they all focused on us. Blatant hilarity replaced the previous somber mood.

"Go girl," said an older man, who had previously told me he had prostate cancer. "Let's see you get that stick up in the air."

Standing there dumbly with the rod at knee height, I had no choice but to spring into action. The now jovial audience cheered as I gamely started the long lift. Patients and visitors alike all shouted encouragement. Even the nurses, hearing the ruckus, joined in.

"Go, go, go," the crowd yelled as I managed to get the stick to my waist.

My husband watched, a big grin showing his delight at what he'd started, and repeated his challenge. "Lift the stick over your head when you're ready for sex."

A cheer rose up from the crowd, and again they chanted, "Go, go, go."

I proceeded like an Olympic contender and raised the rod parallel to my chest.

"You can do better," someone in the back of the room roared.

You bet I could. Grunting, I lifted the rod to shoulder height.

"Go, go, go," they hollered.

My arm felt so stiff. Could I possibly get this thing over my head? And was I really ready for sex?

Both actions remained questionable. Then again, how could I disappoint my fans?

Concentrating with all my might, I willed that left arm to go up, up, up . . . until I held the rod over my head, as high as it could go. Talk about triumph. My fellow patients whistled, stamped, and shouted themselves hoarse. What a great afternoon!

Dean came toward me for a bear hug, forgetting all about my very sore chest. I had to push him away. Displaying his naughty grin, he took my hand and led me out and to my room. Of course, the very public hospital was not conducive to romance. All we did was talk. Still, I knew my fans in the lounge got a kick out of the closed door. Besides, the doctor promised I could leave the bustling hospital for the privacy of my own home the next day, drains and all.

Some years have gone by since my bout with breast cancer. I still feel the same way I did that afternoon when I held that rod high over my head. I'd beaten cancer, and everything would turn out all right.

—*Petrina Aubol*

From To-Do to Ta-Da!

T hings to Do Before I Die.

We all have a list like that, don't we? For a breast cancer survivor, such a list takes on new meaning. My list isn't totally outside the realm of possibility. Okay, I probably won't ever climb Mount Everest, but I surely will get my attic cleaned out—some day. This is a story of how breast cancer made it possible for me to check off one item on my list.

I was diagnosed with breast cancer at age forty-nine, exactly the age my mother was when she was diagnosed—and it wasn't a surprise to me. The possibility that I, too, would one day battle breast cancer had always been in the back of my mind. Unlike my mother, though, at the time I was diagnosed I was obese (weighing in excess of 230 pounds), sedentary, and pre-diabetic. I hadn't always been heavy; the weight had gradually crept up after the birth of my two daughters. Now, on top of the health risks the obesity brought, I also had another, potentially life-threatening and certainly life-changing, health issue to deal with. As it turns out, being diagnosed with breast cancer not only changed my life, it also saved my life.

Initially, of course, I experienced the usual anger, sadness, and helplessness that all breast cancer patients go through. But after I'd successfully completed the first round of treatment—a lumpectomy and radiation—those emotions faded, and I got back to my normal life for the next couple of years.

Like many survivors, I read everything I could get my hands on about breast cancer. Just the words "breast cancer" in a headline or title grabbed my attention. I felt I had done what I could for my cancer. I went through the recommended treatment and was taking tamoxifen. I didn't smoke or drink; and I continued to get regular mammograms. Then I read a line in an article that shocked and scared me: Being obese can increase your risk of recurrent breast cancer by more than 40 percent, especially if you gained the weight as an adult. I had never equated my lifestyle with an increased breast cancer risk. Sure, I knew that obesity was putting me at increased risk for diabetes, heart disease, and orthopedic problems—but breast cancer? I had no idea.

So, then and there, I decided it was time to make a serious change in my life and to try to regain some control over my health. I enlisted the support of a wonderful physician and his team (nurse, nutritionist, and exercise physiologist) to help me do it. We developed a plan that would become my routine for life. It wasn't radical; I was simply taught to make responsible and healthy food choices and encouraged to exercise. Within a few weeks of beginning the program, my lab tests showed significant improvements with respect to glucose levels and fats in my blood, and within four months, all my labs were normal and I had lost thirty pounds. I was no longer at risk for diabetes, and my risk for serious cardiac incident had been cut dramatically. But I still had a long way to go.

My exercise of choice was walking. I started out slowly, gradually increasing my pace until one day I was power walking. From time to time, one of my daughters would accompany me on my walks, and I'll never forget the day—and my own sense of accomplishment—when a very fit, seventeen-year-old asked *me* to slow down! Then I joined a gym; I was getting serious now. One day on the treadmill, walking just didn't seem to be enough, and I started to jog. That day, I was thrilled to jog one mile on the treadmill. My face was red, my breathing hard, and my legs tired, but I did it. The next time, I ran two miles, and before I knew it, I wasn't walking on the treadmill at all but jogging every time.

That's when I realized it might be possible for me to actually complete that item on my "things to do before I die" list: *run*, not walk, the Susan G. Komen Race for the Cure®. I'd been participating in the race for years, well before I was diagnosed with breast cancer, but I'd always walked the 3.2 miles. I wanted to be one of those athletes up front, pushing off the start line when the race began, and to feel the rush of adrenalin as I competed against other runners. But now I told myself, *You're not an athlete, just a middle-aged woman who jogs a little.* So I continued to participate in the race by walking with a large group of friends. At the start of every race, though, I secretly wished I was running.

After two years of lifestyle changes, I had lost sixty-five pounds and was quite fit for a fifty-six-year-old woman. I was exercising regularly and eating a healthy diet. I was happy with my health and proud to set an example for my daughters. I felt in control of my body and certain that I was doing all I could to prevent recurrence of breast cancer.

In the spring of 2007, the local Race for the Cure organization chose me to represent northeastern Ohio at the National Race for the Cure in Washington, D.C. I was honored to participate and excited to attend the race in our nation's capitol. Did I walk that race? No. I ran it! Crossing that finish line was one of the most thrilling moments in my life. I *ran* the National Race for the Cure!

Had I never been diagnosed with breast cancer, today I might find myself still obese and at a much higher risk of, if not actually having had, diabetes, heart disease, and a recurrence of breast cancer. I firmly believe that breast cancer was the wake-up call I needed to change my life—and that changing my life saved my life. Oh, I still haven't managed to clean out the attic yet. Staying healthy and doing other more fun things now top my new list of "Things to Do While I'm Alive and Kicking"— which I intend to be for a very long time.

—*Kathleen Griswold*

Missing Parts

The men just didn't seem to last very long in our family. In addition to his crooked grin, my father left his stamp on all four of his kids by nicknaming our mother Boo. On my thirteenth birthday, too soon after my father died, I watched from the hallway as my nineteen-year-old brother slung a green duffle bag across his thin shoulders, tilted his enlisted man's cap low, and kissed Boo goodbye.

Boo worked overtime as a counselor at the Florence Crittendon Home for Unwed Mothers and rushed home to throw together a dry dinner of meatballs and peas for us three sisters, who never had the heart to complain. In a simple act of tenderness, Betsy, the oldest, flipped through the dusty Betty Crocker cookbook on the top of the fridge and taught herself to cook. From then on, Boo's face lit up every time she stepped into the kitchen and smelled Betsy's sizzling onions, baked chicken, or fresh sliced cucumbers.

Catharine—the tall, skinny one—cleaned the house with regulated vengeance, fuming at my kicked-off sandals and rolling across my bare toes with the vacuum cleaner. Chased out of the house, I fiddled around in the garage. I changed the bicycle tires in the spring, mowed the lawn in the summer, and shaved down the tree stump at Christmas. I discovered the closet where the fuse box hid, how to change the toilet flapper, and what sparked the red and black battery clamps under the hood of Boo's unreliable old station wagon.

Most Sundays, Boo invited two teenaged mothers-to-be from the Crittendon Home over for Betsy's roast beef. Standing in the foyer shaking their umbrellas, the guests offered shy help in the kitchen, while more of Boo's relatives burst in from the back porch. In a house full of obliging females, men seemed to be the missing parts here, but the women seemed to find ways to do without them. These Sundays, their hands were full of bowls of garlicky succotash, collard greens, and buttermilk biscuits. Never-married Aunt Lydia always brought a gallon jug of Mogen David, thumping it down on the kitchen counter. The pregnant girls from the home sat across the table from my grandmothers, two elderly widows who counted their pennies. Lenore, stiff and disapproving, glared over at the protruding young bellies, but Maude, Depression-era generous, passed more biscuits their way. I sat in the middle of it all and listened.

As we ate, Aunt Lydia told her movie star stories. Sixty-one-year-old Lydia, a United Artists film booker, wrapped her thinning hair in a stiff white turban and never left the house without rouge on her face. Every day from her downtown Atlanta cubicle, she talked on the phone to people in Hollywood while she blew smoke rings into the air from a black cigarette holder. She had seen both Elvis and Liberace up close, and Liberace, she claimed, wore high heels. Whenever Lydia spoke, the back of my neck began to tingle with an excitement I could not yet name. On these Sundays, toward the end of each meal, Betsy kicked open the kitchen door and carried out her sugary key lime pie, bringing a longed-for taste of sensuality to all of us.

One Sunday in the spring of 1967, we sisters learned that Lydia would be staying with us for a month while Boo went to the hospital to have the cancer removed from her breasts. Overnight, Lydia moved into our lives, eager to do what she could for us, even if it meant cooking.

Her first night with us, Lydia pushed her fork around a TV dinner tray and tossed back her second bourbon and Coke. She looked into the kitchen and noticed the liquor was running low. "Come on, baby," she said to me, "I got to get me something at the pharmacy."

Driving through the city's congested streets, I sat on the creamy leather front seat of my aunt's sedan and listened to jazz on the radio. Aunt Lydia stamped hard on the gas, gunning the heavy Impala along Peachtree Street. She drove with her left hand on the wheel and lit a cigarette with her free hand. At the red light, she came to a full halt and turned to me with a sigh. A tendril of dyed red hair had escaped Lydia's white turban and dangled along the edge of her peachy cheekbone. It reminded me of the last Christmas Eve my father was alive, when Lydia had walked into our living room wearing a black silk turban and dragging a white fur coat, dragging it slow like a movie star. Snuggling up next to the fireplace, Lydia had nursed an endless glass of champagne and left her sunglasses on during the gift swap.

Now, waiting at the light, Lydia reached over and tapped a pointy red fingernail over my lips. "You know, darlin', you got your daddy's wide mouth. And he was a good-looking man with a real sweetness about him."

I stared at Aunt Lydia's tight head wrap and the smoke line trailing from the cigarette holder clinched in her teeth. The ash on her cigarette was a full inch long. I waited for it to fall. The familiar description of my father didn't interest me much, because I'd heard it too many times. But watching Aunt Lydia handle that cigarette holder thrilled me. I had hardly even thought about Boo being in the hospital—until Aunt Lydia grabbed my hand and pressed it tight against my cheek.

"Don't you worry about your momma now," Aunt Lydia told me. "She's going to be fine. Just fine." But the wrinkled skin at the corners of Lydia's eyes was wet and her voice shook.

With a start I realized that I hadn't missed my mother at all. But in that moment, for the first time, I saw fragile Aunt Lydia wasn't anything like a movie star and never would be. Aunt Lydia released my hand onto the seat beside her and patted it, patted it, with her knotty old fingers. A wave of nausea back-washed through my throat, leaving me sick with fear of losing all the women I'd ever loved.

Ten days later, Boo came home from the hospital. I was glad to see her standing there in the foyer, gaunt and bald with a done-in smile on her face. Catharine hung back against the wall, afraid to touch her mother. Betsy took Boo's arm and helped her climb into the four-poster bed, where she slept on her back straight through for eleven hours, not moving once.

The first time I saw Boo step naked out of the shower, dripping wet and nearly hairless, I thought she looked like she had her head on backward. With her scooped-out chest, the thin red scars left by the scalpel could have been Boo's shoulder blades. Her pubic area had a forgotten, ancient history look to it. This would take some getting used to. None of us girls said much about it, but Betsy came up with a plan.

She got up early the next Saturday morning and caught the bus downtown. "Going shopping," she said.

Four hours later, she returned with a package the size of a small shoebox, set it down on the piano bench, and called everyone into the living room. A trace of our father's wide smile stretched across her face as she beamed over her selection. She winked over Boo's shoulder at Catharine and me. "Take a look, Boo."

Boo lifted the box top and peered inside. We sisters leaned in, too. Nestled there against the pink satin cloth were two nipple-less plastic mounds. They looked like putty-colored tennis balls sliced in half. They were fake breasts to be placed inside Boo's lonely old brassiere.

"Well?" Betsy bounced on the balls of her feet and asked into the long silence. "What d'ya think?"

I stared into the box and shrugged, leaving my shoulders up in the air. Catharine scooped up one of the mounds and held it close to Boo's pale face for a moment. She rolled her eyeballs like they'd just been oiled. "This is not the color of skin." Jiggling the Jell-O-like thing, she plopped it back on the pink satin cloth next to its twin.

We three girls looked back and forth from Boo's face to the boxed set of make-believe breasts, waiting for a response from Boo.

Boo screwed her mouth into a perplexed pucker and crossed her arms over her flat chest. She stared down at the lifeless forms in the box and nodded. "They'll do," she said

A tall, handsome woman, Boo had an absent-minded way of misplacing her new breasts, and they began to turn up in unexpected places. I moved carefully around them at the bathroom sink, left stacked together as Boo had bent down to brush her teeth. Outside on the back porch, Betsy discovered a roguish singlet, where it had popped out when Boo bent to feed the dog. That first winter, the left breast had to be fished out of the floor heater quickly with a coat hanger, before it melted.

One afternoon at the intersection of Lullwater and Ponce de Leon, Boo sailed the old station wagon right through a red light. The thrust of her down-shift into second had sent Boo's right breast flying, momentarily distracting her. Frozen in the passenger seat, Catharine stared in terror as she watched the loose maiden roll around the floorboard and wedge itself snug under the brake pedal. The only other car present that particular afternoon had a flashing blue light.

When summer came around that year, our family of women rented a house at the seashore to celebrate I don't know what. On a white-hot afternoon, I dog-paddled along in the waves as Boo drifted out past the whitecaps. In a lazy back float, Boo's long, flat form rose and fell with the seesaw rhythm of the current. I understood my mother's body was less perfect than most, but I'd come to believe it was in some way more full, somehow freed from life's known blueprint. That afternoon I wasn't surprised when one of Boo's putty-colored breast forms coasted by me atop a good-sized wave. Quick as a water spider, I let loose a few kicks, grabbed the seagoing maiden, and swam back to shore with it. I knew my mother could manage fine enough without her missing parts.

When I stepped onto the sand, I turned back toward the distant figure and called out, scattering the shorebirds into the tide. "Boo, come on in! You're out too far!"

But Boo didn't care to hear my voice over the high-pitched cries of the gulls.

I settled in between my sisters under the shade of a wide umbrella stuck in the sand. Tossing Boo's renegade breast idly back and forth in my hands like a hackeysack, I focused on my mother's long, flat body way out there among the waves. My sisters and I watched together in silence as our mother rolled over and swam out still farther past the whitecaps, then flipped onto her back to float longer in the buoyant water. As we leaned forward into the distance between us, we saw Boo raise a long-legged salute and wiggle her toes in our direction, quite content to ride, unanchored and weightless, alone in the sea.

—Glen Finland

Timing Is Everything

My husband always says timing in life is everything. Usually, he is referring to a driver pulling out of a prize parking spot just as we approach. I'm sure he never anticipated my getting a call-back on my mammogram during October, Breast Cancer Awareness month. First came the more enhanced mammogram, followed by an ultrasound. These uncomfortable procedures were made all the more anxiety-provoking by the running commentary. "I know it's there, but I can't quite find it. I can tell you it's very small and very deep." This did not inspire confidence.

The doctor offered three options: (1) wait a few months, (2) do a needle biopsy, or (3) do a breast MRI. I let the doctor decide; he seemed more qualified. He chose the MRI, which had to be scheduled by my primary care physician, who was vacationing in Italy. That meant another week of waiting, but at least we were approaching the end of October; I was already as aware of breast cancer as I wished to be.

The MRI was a surreal experience. If I had retained one shred of dignity up to that point, it was gone now. You want me to put my what, where? Fortunately, someone had described it, so I wasn't totally surprised when I was asked to lie on my stomach and allow my breasts to fall into two holes on the table while an intravenous fluid ran in my arm.

Next, the surgeon reaffirmed the diagnosis. My husband accompanied me on that visit. Until then, he had been comfortably living in the land of denial. Sometimes, I joined him there. It's a nice place to visit.

"You're a good candidate for a lumpectomy, followed by radiation," the doctor said.

"No chemo?" I whispered.

"No," he assured me. "You could be the poster child for early detection. This is not what you'll die from."

Did he know something I didn't?

The biopsy was scheduled for two days before Thanksgiving, when sixteen people were coming for dinner. There's that impeccable timing again. The procedure was relatively painless, but unfortunately, I was allergic to the surgical dressing, so Thanksgiving was an uncomfortable day. I had plenty of help, and if anyone noticed that I was wiped out by the end of the day, they were too polite to mention it.

I had decided not to tell the family until after the holiday, so on Saturday I gathered up the women: two daughters, one daughter-in-law, and two of my many granddaughters. They were empathetic, concerned, encouraging. This is a subject women know well. I have discovered that if you tell a woman, "I have a lump," they don't say, "Where?" One daughter assured me that God had a plan for me. I was sure He had, but was I going to like it?

My oldest son called me after hearing the news. "What exactly are they going to do?" he asked.

"They're going to take out the lump, and then I'll have six weeks of radiation."

"That's enough for me," he said.

My youngest son e-mailed, "That really sucks!"

That night I e-mailed every woman in my address book: friends, nieces, sisters-in-law, every one. I called them my "Ya-Yas," told them to get their mammograms, and promised to update them through the whole procedure, which I did. Not a day went by that a note of love and encouragement was not in my inbox.

The next week it was back to the surgeon. This time our daughter, Susan, accompanied us. She sat up on the table and took notes. My husband retreated a little farther. The doctor advised that I see the oncologist and let her make a plan of treatment. And another week went by.

The oncologist was a personable young woman. She highly recommended the surgeon and his opinion on a course of action: surgery, radiation, and then five years of medication. Before we left, we made the appointment for surgery, December 11. Everyone agreed I'd be fine by Christmas.

The weekend before the surgery we went to Long Island, New York, to visit my ninety-nine-year-old mother in the nursing home. Needless to say, I did not tell her. She is totally alert and in good health, but her world is very small; best to leave it that way. I did tell my sister and her daughter. We did not have a history of breast cancer in the family. We do now.

The day of surgery, we were at the hospital by seven in the morning, which is not my shining hour. I must say that everyone, without exception, I had dealt with had been kind and compassionate. That morning was no exception.

The surgeon popped in just as I was drifting off. "I'll be removing the lump and several lymph nodes," he told me. "I don't expect any node involvement, but if there is, we will have to go back in."

I was happy to disappear into the anesthesia. I woke up to a little pain but severe nausea, and was immediately medicated for both. Within an hour or so I was ready to go home. The nurse gave me half a pain pill for the road and a prescription for twenty more. The surgeon had told my husband all had gone well, and there were no surprises. That sounded encouraging.

Once home, I ensconced myself in the recliner and drifted off. The nausea did not abate, so food was out of the question. Later, in bed, sleep was difficult. I couldn't sleep on either side, until I finally tucked a pillow under the bad arm. In the morning, I took a pain pill, and the whole room started to spin. So it was Tylenol after that.

I was beginning to think that my being fine by Christmas was a slight exaggeration. But by the twenty-first, I felt well enough to go back to the school where I volunteer with first graders. They had made me combined holiday and get-well cards. They presented them one by one with smiles and hugs, and I tucked them into a holiday bag they had decorated. One of the boys pressed his card into my hand with such a determined expression that I opened it immediately. The front had a blue tree with an orange star on top. Inside it said,

> "*Dear Mrs. Coddy,*
> *We mess you. Hop you are felling bitter.*
> *Luv, Carlos*"

I rubbed the top of his crew cut. "I missed you too, Carlos."

A follow-up visit to the surgeon confirmed that the surgery had gone as planned and the nodes were clear. Christmas actually did go quite well, because I didn't have to pretend that there was nothing wrong. We skirted the issue nicely and had a pleasant day.

Then we headed back to the oncologist, who was elated to tell me I was now cancer-free. She may have noticed I was less enthusiastic than she was. I thought, *I've been cancer-free for seventy-two years and had hoped to stay that way.* She scheduled six weeks of radiation, five days a week. Then would come the medication, because my cancer was hormone-receptor positive . . . a good thing. Who knew?

But here we go with the timing again: I was to start radiation at the end of January, prime snow time in our area.

"Don't worry if you miss a session," the oncologist assured me. "We'll just tack it on at the end."

Very reassuring.

Radiation meant going to a hospital about a half hour away, because our local hospital did not offer it. When I checked in at registration, I asked for directions to radiology.

"Just go down one floor. It's right next to the morgue."

Thank you so much.

The first visit was with the radiologist to outline the treatment plan. The second was for a CAT scan to pinpoint the exact spot so as not to injure the heart. That appointment included making five tiny tattoos for future reference. I thought of my son, who has extensive tattooing. He must be insane!

Radiation started the next day, and as promised, it was a non-event, ten minutes of a formidable machine maneuvering overhead, making a rattling noise similar to the bingo machines in Florida. The attending nurse advised me that the most common side effects are a sunburn-like rash and extreme fatigue.

"I'm a very low-energy person" I told her. "I might not even notice the fatigue."

She looked me square in the eyes. "You'll notice."

I was instructed not to shave my underarms nor wear standard deodorants, because they contain aluminum. I was to apply unscented lotion.

"Oh, and by the way, you can't wear a polyester bra. You need to get all cotton or, better still, wear a cotton undershirt. You can put your bra over it if you'd feel more comfortable."

Now, there's the look I was going for. Fortunately, sweatshirts cover a multitude of fashion faux pas. I discovered that natural deodorant smelled like a cross between a pine forest and a fungus. I was waiting for the grandchildren to ask why Grandma smelled like a swamp.

In the waiting room I made the acquaintance of two women. After a few days we had formed a mini-support group, sharing our painful and scary experiences along with the funny ones. Paula had extensive surgery, followed by chemo and now radiation. She made me count my blessings, but when I told her my experience was minimal compared to hers, she took my hand and said, "It's still cancer, and sometimes that reality will just hit you." Amen to that. Jane's experience was similar to mine, but she was a much younger woman, young enough to be my daughter.

By the third week we were so bonded that the technicians hated to interrupt us for treatment. They told us that in the men's waiting room, the gentlemen do not exchange a word and barely make eye contact. They might have to "share" something. It reinforced my theory: Women are amazing.

The truth about radiation therapy is that the hardest part, for me, anyway, was getting there every day. My timing made it the coldest part of a New England winter, the months we usually spend in the Florida sunshine. Undressing and redressing took longer than the actual treatment, especially with my bra over my undershirt. I never did develop much of a rash. I was told not to wear a bikini this year. Like that was going to happen.

The other ladies finished a week before I did. I felt bereft when they left me. I knew I would never see them again. You take your sisters where and when you find them. When I finally finished, I began on the medication, which was extraordinarily expensive and had myriad side effects. But I found that popping that tiny pill in my mouth made me feel empowered. I was doing something proactive for my health.

It has been a year since my diagnosis. I will be followed closely for the next few years.

When people ask me what was most difficult about having breast cancer, I answer, "Telling my daughters."

Last week I had my yearly mammogram. I must admit, I was anxious, but the doctor said the magic words, "You're fine." And I am. I immediately emailed the Ya-Yas. God is good.

—Joan A. Cody

Never Say Never

I feel a sudden swirling in my belly, and the reality hits me like a ton of bricks. A life is growing inside me.

The anxiety quickly subsides and is replaced by an eager anticipation that lights my soul. I am having a baby after breast cancer.

This little miracle of life has not come easy. The five-year journey leading here has been filled with times of shock and suffering. But for every moment of pain, there has been one of joy; for every moment of worry, there has been one of hope. Ultimately, this experience has taught me to live for today, to not sweat the small stuff (or at least try not to), and to be the positive person I need to be—for myself, for my family, and for my "pink ribbon" sisters.

My son was three when I was diagnosed with invasive ductal carcinoma. Only weeks before, I had miscarried and was still agonizing over the loss—wondering, as many women who've miscarried do, whether it was somehow my fault. When the new doctor who was replacing my family doctor called to schedule an appointment with me, it did not seem out of the ordinary and, in fact, wasn't. It was simply a doctor wanting to check up on a new patient who had recently suffered a miscarriage. Only in retrospect, years later, did I realize that her phone call, prompted by the miscarriage, had changed and perhaps saved my life.

When I was nursing my son I'd developed mastitis, and my left breast had become hard, inflamed, and painful. The infection was successfully treated with antibiotics, but for some unknown reason, the pain never left. I began to guard that breast from the leaps and bounds of my active toddler. I asked my general practitioner about the lingering pain on more than one occasion, but the concerns I expressed led to no further testing. "You have lumpy breast tissue," "Cancer doesn't hurt," "You are too young for breast cancer," I was told.

So life went on. We got caught up in work and family obligations, bought a minivan and a new home, and doted on our growing little boy. Then, we were overjoyed to learn I was pregnant again. A new baby would make our lives complete! But it was not to be. I lost the baby at thirteen weeks.

After my former doctor's indifferent bedside manner, I was surprised to learn that the new doctor's primary reason for seeing me was simply to lend support. She had received the report of my quick and final trip to the hospital emergency room. "You lost a lot of blood," she said during my appointment. "It must have been very traumatic for you. Do you have someone to talk to?" That she understood how important it is for a woman who has miscarried to have someone to share her fears, sadness, and guilt with, someone to talk to, comforted me greatly.

Talking with the doctor opened up a new line of trust, and I felt compelled to share my concern about the pain in my breast. Although my former doctor had assured me it was of no concern each time I'd asked, I figured it couldn't hurt to get another opinion. Besides, it nagged at me, and I was now sure I could feel a lump.

And so the whirlwind of tests—and then treatments—began.

My doctor had tears in her eyes when she told me, "You have breast cancer."

Five years later, I am still here, currently cancer-free . . . and five months pregnant with a baby girl. The body I felt had failed me is now the source of life. Against tough odds, we are bringing another child into the world. As our daughter thrives inside my body, fear and despair have been transformed into hope and joy, and I am fierce with determination to raise both my son and my daughter to adulthood. The baby kicks hard as if to remind me of her presence. Like her mommy, she is strong—a fighter. But even I didn't know my strength and resolve when I was first diagnosed with breast cancer. Then, I was afraid I wouldn't see my son go to kindergarten and I was still grieving over the baby I'd lost.

The chemo treatments began about the time I would have been preparing for the birth of the child I'd miscarried. Every time the intravenous for the chemo drugs went in, I felt my fertility being ripped from my body. When the surgeon said "no more babies," his words had torn my heart in two. My husband had looked at me in defeat, but he assured me that one child was fine and he vowed we would get through this.

It wasn't fair. This was not how we had planned our lives. Breast cancer was turning my world upside down, and I bitterly resented it. I yearned for another child, not just for me and my husband but also for our son. As an only child, I had grown up wishing for a sister to laugh with or a brother to admire.

So the crib stayed in storage, the baby clothes packed away, and the nursery walls unpainted. As it turned out, removing the lump was not enough. The cancer was very aggressive and had spread to the lymph nodes, several of which were then also removed. Six rounds of chemotherapy and thirty-three rounds of radiation treatment took its toll. I lost thirty pounds, all of my hair, and all but a sliver of hope of giving birth again.

Nevertheless, two years after the diagnosis and a year after treatment ended, my husband and I decided to try again. When the pregnancy test was positive, I didn't know whether to laugh or cry. We wanted a baby desperately, but we feared a recurrence of the breast cancer, so my husband and I rejoiced quietly, filled with anxiety. I confided the news to the director of cancer care, with whom I had become close, and she insisted that I tell my oncologist—which I did, in a broom closet of the oncology center. My doctors were overjoyed, and I got caught up in their excitement as well as my own.

But, again, I miscarried, this time at seven weeks—despite my cancer scans being clear. Bewildered, but not beaten, we resigned ourselves that this pregnancy, too, was not meant to be. As we mourned the loss of now two babies, faced the possibility of having no more children, and confronted the constant risk of my breast cancer recurring, it seemed as though our friends were celebrating their abundance in both health and family. Though I was glad for them, their good fortune made me even more sad about our misfortune—and envious. I kept lamenting, *Why is this happening to me? Will I ever be able to carry another child to term? Will the cancer return? When will things be "normal" again? When will this rollercoaster end? I am ready to get off this ride!*

I'm not quite sure when it happened or whether it happened slowly or suddenly, but at one point "Why me?" changed to "Why not me?" Why should I not be among the one in every eight women in this country with breast cancer? Why should I not be one of the millions who survived—and went on to raise their children and even to give birth? When this new perspective finally came to me, I wanted to stand on the tallest peak and shout: "I am a survivor!"

At about that time, I met a survivor of stage four breast cancer at a conference in Toronto. Years before her diagnosis, she had given birth to her last child at age forty-two. Though I was in the child-bearing prime of my life and my cancer scans were clear, I was beginning to believe that I would never have another child. She looked me in the eyes and told me to hold on to hope, that miracles do happen. I believed her.

I realized then that I had another purpose, above and beyond living to raise my son and, God willing, to give birth to and raise another child, too. And that was to share my experience with—to educate and empower—other young women who were going through this journey, too. Young women do get breast cancer, and they need to know they are not alone, that others have and are going through it—and surviving.

I rub my growing belly. Our little angel of hope will arrive in four months—in the spring, the perfect time for a new beginning. We have named her Taryn, and my husband has honored me by suggesting that her middle name be the same as mine. He was right all along. We got through it, and today we're the better for it.

Five years ago, I despaired over our empty nursery and the hole in our hearts. Now, I ponder whether bright pink or soft pink is the better choice for our daughter's nursery. Soon, I will unpack the bins of baby things that have been stored in the garage for eight years. And as I decorate Taryn's room with butterflies, dragonflies, and a rocking chair that sits in the corner, I envision rocking our little miracle to sleep. She will gaze into my eyes and find comfort in my voice and my touch. I will smell her sweet scent and wonder at this incredible blessing in my life. I will watch her and her brother grow up. I will watch her fall in love with my husband, and I will watch my son take her under his wing. Life is wonderful.

—*Allison Jean Roberts*

Dancing in the Moonlight

I've never had breast cancer, but I'd like to tell you the story of someone who has—a woman who not only survived, but who, eleven years later, celebrated her fiftieth wedding anniversary by strolling the sunny plazas of Venice and watching the stars brighten the night sky in Greece. It's a tale of courage and hope, a story I know well. You see, that stargazer is my mother.

It was early summer, 1995. Mom and I were talking on the phone. After chatting about this and that, she casually said, "They think things look a little suspicious, so they're keeping an eye on it."

Who's keeping an eye on what? I wondered, a snippet of anxiety flitting through my mind. *The president is keeping an eye on the nation? The neighbor is keeping an eye on his tennis-shoe-stealing puppy? My dad is keeping an eye on his ripening tomatoes?*

"I'm not sure what you're talking about," I said.

"The doctor," Mom said. "During my breast exam, he thought things seemed a little suspicious. He wants to check it again in a couple of months."

After the initial shock, I talked myself out of worrying. *The doctor wasn't moving quickly on it, and Mom didn't sound upset. It was probably just a cyst, right? She'd had those before. Surely, she didn't have cancer now. Her immune system couldn't be that big a catastrophe.*

My mom's mind is as sharp as a straight pin. She can tell you every card that's been played in a half-finished game of gin rummy. And when I was a kid, she could beat me at a game of jacks before I even bounced that little red ball. Speaking of straight pins, she can sew like a whiz and made most of my clothes when I was young. Shorts, tops, and my favorite lavender gingham Easter dress with a lilac, satin ribbon had all been sewn by my mom's hand, just for me.

But her body is a wreck. If there was ever a woman born falling apart, it was Roberta Kieliger. She had a history of neck, back, uterine, and ovarian problems. As my dad liked to say, "Your mother is an illness waiting to happen."

After the initial news of the suspicious breast exam, the months flew by—mostly because we didn't realize just how concerned we should be. Then,

Mom's doctor retired. At her next checkup, a new physician was on board.

"The doctor did a biopsy," my mom said to me on the phone. "There's cancer, and they're going to do the surgery in November."

The whole world seemed to tip upside down. There was nothing for me to do but dig my fingernails in and hang on.

Mom continued, "I'd like you to be here. Will you fly out for the surgery?" A note of pleading had entered her voice.

"Don't ask me to come," I said, but not because I didn't want to go. *I want you to know I care without you asking for it; give me the chance to show that I won't let you go through this without me by your side,* I thought. "Let me offer to come before you ask," I said.

"Okay," she replied.

"Do you want me to come out?" I asked, as if I didn't already know the answer.

"Yes," she responded, as if she hadn't already asked it of me before.

It was a crazy, mixed-up conversation, but life was suddenly crazy and mixed up, and somehow, the flow of what we'd said made logical sense to us.

"Ma, how far along is . . . um . . . it?" The word "cancer" was stuck somewhere in my brain synapses, and I just couldn't get it out. Or didn't want to say it out loud. That would've made it too real.

"I'll send you the lab report," she said.

When the report came, my husband, Russ, gave it to a physician friend and asked his opinion. Russ didn't tell me until the night before I was scheduled to leave that it was a stage two, grade three infiltrating ductal carcinoma, and the prognosis was poor. My heart pounded and my ears rang at the news. Sleep was long in coming as my mind processed the terrifying possibilities.

I flew out the next morning, and my folks met me at the airport. We tried for the next several days to act as if everything were normal. But how could it be? When someone is diagnosed with cancer, normal flies out the window.

The morning of the surgery, I got up at four o'clock to get a drink. My mom cracked open her bedroom door to see if I needed anything.

Swallowing a sip of cool water from the glass in my hand, I asked, "Are you okay? Why are you awake?"

"I heard you get up."

"Go back to sleep," I said, trying to sound cheerful. Then off the cuff I added, "Or Santa won't come."

Who in their right mind equates cancer surgery with Santa arriving? I could have kicked myself.

Chalk it up to a gal who was so stressed she was putting thoughts together Dr. Seuss-style.

My dad and I checked Mom into the hospital with smiles pasted on our faces.

As they prepped her for surgery, she said, "After they take me to the operating room, don't wait around—go get something to eat. It'll be awhile before I wake up."

As they wheeled her away on the gurney, we waved a forced, cheery goodbye and promised we'd see her later. Watching her disappear down the hall, I wanted to kick the barren walls, throw the squat-ugly visitor's chair through the window, and smash everything in sight. Instead, we walked out the door and drove to a restaurant.

My dad and I chatted the whole time . . . about absolutely nothing. He's the silent type when it comes to emotions. I realized he was feeling numb, just like me.

After eating, we went back to the hospital and waited for the news. Finally, the doctor came out and told us she'd removed all the cancer and my mom was in recovery. We spent the rest of the day visiting with Mom, but she was too groggy to remember anything. She'd wake up, ask how things went, fall back asleep, and then wake up and ask the same questions again.

By bedtime, my dad and I were back at my folks' house. Despite the exhaustion, I didn't sleep any better that night. Mixed-up dreams filled with snatches of fear had me tossing and turning until the wee hours of the morning. I should have known the nightmares were a premonition.

The next day, the phone rang, and my heart flip-flopped and my mind raced. *What if it's bad news? Don't answer it! Wait. It's probably Mom, saying she's able to come home. Quick, answer it!*

Dad picked up the receiver, and I heard him say, "Hi. How're you feeling? You're not going to be able to come home today? But the doctor said you'd only have to be in overnight. What's going on?"

Although the cancer was gone, my mom's system was still a catastrophe. The incision wouldn't heal, and everything in the area had turned deep purple, inching into black. You didn't have to be a doctor to know that was a bad sign. They kept her in the hospital several extra days, gave her oxygen, antibiotics, and everything else they could. Finally, a specialist determined the problem. He pronounced, "She's got a delicate blood supply."

Only my mom—the person who was an illness waiting to happen—could go in with a cancer diagnosis and come out with something new.

After several days, she was allowed to go home. That was followed with six months of treatments—chemotherapy that made her sick to her stomach and caused her hair to fall out. She wore a cute denim hat to boost morale, and all three of us managed to live through the chemo.

It's been twelve years now since Mom's surgery and chemotherapy. She's an active member of the Pink Ladies, a breast cancer survivor group in Charles County, Maryland. Not only that, but because she understands the heartbreak and fear, she's been asked to form a new breast cancer support group for seniors in her home town of La Plata.

I never wanted my mother to be a breast cancer patient, but she was. I desperately wanted her to live through it, and she did. We've been very lucky and extremely blessed.

Someday soon, Mom plans on taking another trip. This time she'll go to Russia, where she says she's going to dance with my dad in the moonlight. Maybe I'll go along and dance with them. After all, she might have been the one with cancer, but all three of us are survivors.

—*C. Lynn Beck*

Breast Cancer, Funny?

"The funny thing, Carol, is that nothing ever hurts," Diane said. "You tend to think something as serious as cancer would hurt, but mine never hurt. Isn't that funny?"

Carol thought it odd that Diane had used the word "funny" twice. Carol didn't think her tumor was funny, and she didn't think Diane meant funny, as in ha-ha. She decided it was just a word people used.

The first funny things she noticed were how her friends reacted when she told them she had a small tumor in her left breast and was undergoing radiation therapy.

"You're so lucky."

"Be glad they got it early."

"Think how much worse it could have been."

"You'll be fine."

"They sure have made remarkable innovations in diagnosis and treatment."

The group called itself "We Survivors." Carol didn't know whether she would be a survivor at the time. She soon realized none of the other women knew whether they'd be survivors either. The radiation would work or it wouldn't. She would not let herself think beyond that.

The leader was Jean, who'd had a bilateral mastectomy seven years ago. Carol couldn't stop looking at Jean's chest.

"We used to call them falsies," Jean said. "Now they're called all sorts of other things, but they're still falsies."

There was a lot of tittering, nervous laughter. Carol thought everyone acted like it was the first day in a new school full of strangers.

Jean said, "We are not going to be a bunch of somber sisters with long faces and barrels of tears. First, if you're married, get over that your husband doesn't know how to act or what to say. Breast cancer is not a guy thing. Second, worrying does no good, ever. Third, trust your doctor. If you don't trust your doctor, get another one. Now I'll tell you my story. It's long and complicated, and if you want to leave right now, go ahead."

Carol looked around and saw a lot of fidgeting, but no one left. Jean told her story as if she were on stage. She ended with what she said was how she now lived. "There's absolutely nothing I or any of you can do about having breast cancer. You have it, you live with it. Period. Then you go on. You go to work. You volunteer. You take walks and smell the flowers and watch the birds. You don't feel sorry for yourself. Or blame yourself. It's not your fault. You laugh. It's the best medicine there is. It makes you feel better, and it makes those around you feel better. This may sound funny, but it's true.

Carol glanced at the woman named Grace, who clearly hadn't expected this sort of pep talk. It appeared Grace hadn't washed her hair for weeks. She was fiddling with her wedding band. She slumped in her chair.

"Does anyone want to talk about their chemo?" Jean asked.

No one did.

"It stinks," Jean said.

More nervous laughter.

"Even my eyelashes went," Jean said. "So what could I do? Die? I wasn't ready for dying. I got through it, and as you can see, I have eyelashes again and hair on my head. Not as much as before, but, what the heck, it's hair."

She didn't look at Grace as she went on. "And I wash my hair and care for it like I didn't do before cancer. Yes, ladies, it's all right to use the C word. I'm not going to look like some sickly middle-aged broad with no makeup and unwashed hair. And another thing, it's about your teeth. We need to brush and floss our teeth, and use whitener, if necessary. You want to look well, not sick."

Carol ran her tongue over her top teeth. *I brush, I floss,* she thought. She saw Grace touch her hair and grimace.

Jean continued. "As for your family, of course it's up to you who you want to tell and who you don't. If you have someone like my Aunt Jane, who had breast cancer, you won't want to tell her, because she'll carry on about how it's genetic and her fault and how sorry she is."

"That's funny," a woman named Charlotte said. "I have an Aunt Jane. She didn't have breast cancer, though. She has arthritis. Isn't it funny how some members of the same family get it and some don't?"

There's that word again, Carol thought. *Funny.*

As the weeks of radiation came to an end, Carol thought increasingly about funny. Tom brought home roses. He'd laughed and said how funny it was that he could go to a florist and get roses in January.

Grace called. She told Carol she'd spent more money than she cared to tell in a hair salon, where she'd had her hair cut, dyed, and straightened. "It's funny," she said. "It makes you feel less cancerous to have a new look."

When Dr. Adams told Carol she would not have to come back to see him for three months, he'd said, "It's funny how this can go. You never know."

Tom turned into a comedian. Carol knew he was doing what he could to keep up her spirits. He came home with jokes. He told her stories about the funny folks in his office—the woman who wore lipstick the color of cotton candy, the new guy who proclaimed himself "an apple addict." When Carol asked what that meant, Tom said the guy walked around carrying an apple all the time because it helped him stop thinking about smoking. Tom told her about his boss who came in one day and announced he was retiring early because he and his wife wanted to travel. Carol thought maybe she and Tom should do that.

When Michelle came to visit, she asked her mother what the pills in the bathroom were for. Carol had forgotten to put them away. "Cholesterol," she said. She thought it rather funny that she could come up with this fib on such short notice.

When she went to fill her prescription for the anti-cancer medicine, the pharmacist did not make eye contact. The first word Carol could think of was funny. She wanted to tell him it was all right.

Three years later, Tom was still telling jokes and making Carol laugh. Michelle still periodically asked her mother how her cholesterol was. And Carol was still working as a receptionist at the real estate company, a job she'd maintained throughout her breast cancer treatments.

Once all the women in the survivors group had gotten to know each other, they talked openly about their fears—of dying, of the cancer returning, of their husbands and boyfriends leaving them.

"What we do is we carry on," Jean said. "We take every single day as a gift. We care for and about other people. We don't mope. We live love."

Carol tried. She couldn't help thinking her tumor might return, might travel somewhere else in her body, might eventually kill her. But she managed to put such thoughts aside and do as Jean said. She smiled at strangers. She read stories to blind people once a week. She went shopping with Michelle to buy a crib; she would be a grandmother in five months.

"It's funny," Michelle said. "I can't think of you as Grandma. You look too young."

Carol laughed and hugged her daughter right there in the store.

Three years and three months after the diagnosis, Carol told Tom it was time they went on vacation somewhere. "An island with aqua sea."

"Funny," he said. "I've been thinking the same thing."

—Barbara Leedom

Bonus Time

I crouch only feet away from the armored vehicle. The pungent odor of gunpowder fills the air. Several SWAT team members, dressed in black and carrying weapons, run close to me and pull on their gas masks. Then, firing through a window, they rush to the red-framed door.

If someone had told me ten years ago that this was how I'd be spending my Wednesday afternoon, I'd have been shocked. I'm almost sixty-three years old. I'm the mother of two kids and the grandmother of four. So how is it that I'm staying low to the ground while six muscular men with a battering ram charge by? Breast cancer and the support group I joined after my diagnosis made me the adventurer I am today.

At the time I was diagnosed, I was the poster child for the Uptight Worriers of America. In learning from my mother, I'd learned from the best. We didn't just worry about whether it was going to rain or the porch light might burn out, we also worried whether we would be crushed by random objects falling from the sky on cloudless nights.

As a lifelong Uptight Worrier, I was often afraid to try new things. What if someone laughed at me? What if I made a fool of myself? What if I failed? I was the proverbial gray mouse, stewing and listing everything that "might" happen in any situation.

But in all lives stuff happens to shake things up and rearrange them in an entirely different order. In my case, that "stuff" was a routine mammogram and the diagnosis of breast cancer.

"Invasive lobular carcinoma," the doctor said.

In all of my scenarios, I'd never considered breast cancer. No one in my family had ever had it. How could this be?

The doctor shrugged. "It happens," he said.

For the first time in my life, I didn't have a plan in place. I wasn't ready.

I underwent surgery, radiation, and chemotherapy—dealing with a blur of worries so numerous I could barely keep up, even as an expert. *What if the cancer came back? What if the doctors weren't watching closely enough? What if . . . ? What if . . . ?*

A nearby hospital offered a breast cancer support group. They met at noon several times a month. It took me a while to get up the nerve, but I needed answers.

The day of the group's next meeting, I took the elevator down to the dim depths of the hospital. The halls were silent and empty. My stomach fluttered like it did on the first day of kindergarten. My footsteps echoed in the hall as I rounded the corner. From behind a closed door I heard laughter.

Taking a deep breath, I pulled open the heavy meeting-room door. Inside were six women sitting around a table, talking and chuckling. Their ages ranged from fifty to seventy or more, and they looked like a group of gray-haired, Florida grandmas who should have had cups of tea in front of them and cookies in their hands instead of meeting about something like cancer in the basement of a hospital. I was still wary, but took a seat and listened quietly. Others soon bustled in and sat down.

"What kind of cancer did you have?" a thin woman with curly hair asked me.

"Breast," I answered, nearly in tears from the stress of it all.

"Oh, we all have that," she said matter-of-factly. The others nodded. "We mean, what kind of breast cancer?"

Remembering my doctor's words, I repeated "invasive lobular."

The woman next to me slapped her hand on the table with a bang. I jumped. "Thank goodness!" she said to me with a grin. "Finally, another invasive lobular. I was the only one until you came. Now there are two of us. Welcome!"

I looked around the table. There were no tears, no boxes of tissues. Maybe these smiling women would understand, after all. I let out the breath I didn't know I'd been holding.

I decided to return for the next meeting and the one after that. As the months passed, I learned much about the disease. I also happily decided that these sweet-looking grandmas were slightly deranged. How else could I explain the inception of something as absurd as the Hoots? "Hoots" was the name of the unruly gang we formed. Initiation was a tough one: a breast cancer diagnosis. As Hoots, we even had a slogan: "We'll never be Hooters, because we're missing a few."

As a gang of grandmas, we were part of a tight sisterhood none of us had wanted to join. We never had to explain ourselves or our emotions to each other, because we all knew what it was like. We exchanged important information about our treatments and doctors, and we cheered each milestone—each finished course of chemotherapy, each successful mammogram, and each discarded wig.

We also decided that if we couldn't control our disease, we would control our reaction to it. Irreverent foolishness was often the order of the day. We were the rowdiest group at the cancer camp sponsored by the hospital auxiliary, banished to the farthest corner of the compound the second year so we wouldn't disturb the others.

We participated in a Relay for Life, raising money for cancer research and sleeping in a tent in the center of the walking track. Beforehand, we had a sewing afternoon, but instead of making quilts or doilies like proper grandmas, we made hats out of bras. We wore these brightly colored symbols, complete with sequins and feathers, throughout the relay event.

We also realized that from the day our cancer was removed, we were living on bonus time. Bonus time! What a wonderful thought. Every new day was one we might have missed had our cancer not been discovered and treated. Bonus time liberated us. One woman joined the troop of hospital clowns. Another got to check out professional baseball players by manning the concession counter. I decided to spend my bonus time doing things I might never have considered before.

And that is how I found myself, camera in hand, covering an international SWAT team competition on that warm Florida November afternoon. Later, I interviewed several of the men for an article that would appear in a police magazine, men who faced unknown danger every day and emerged stronger and better equipped to handle what life throws at them, much like the breast cancer survivors I know.

More than nine years later—that's 3,330 days of bonus time and counting!—I'm living unchained and free. My old self wouldn't even recognize the adventurer I've become since joining the Hoots. I'm no longer a timid gray mouse; I've become fearless and bold, sometimes even a little silly. After all, I've already worn a bra hat in public. I'm also no longer a member of the Uptight Worriers of America. I don't have time for nonsense like that. Instead, I strive to fill my time with the things I've always wanted to do. If I fail at something, so what? It won't be the end of the world.

The Hoots continue to get together a few times a year for a meal and a laugh. We're all still here. Nine years. Fourteen women. Cancer survivors all.

I wouldn't recommend breast cancer as the best vehicle to reinvent yourself. But you can skip that step and start spending your bonus time now, before your choices are tugged at by fate. Find your Hoots, lean on them, and become the adventurer you could be. Start today.

—*Michele Ivy Davis*

The Hoopla about Hair

I've always been the kind of woman who can walk into a party unnoticed. People continue to sip their drinks and spin their stories as I scan the crowd for someone I know. As the music wafts through the conversations, it occurs to me that if I turn around and walk out, not a soul will miss me—unless someone was planning to corner me and ask me to volunteer on another committee or cook something for the next party. My gifts to the world lie beneath, rather than displayed on, my surface.

I always assumed if I were beautiful (like the magazines define it) and more shapely (had bigger breasts) a party entrance might be different. But perhaps not. Breast cancer has taught me the secret to getting attention might not be any of those things; instead, it's all up to your head, or rather, what's on your head. Gorgeous hair gets attention, and I found my dazzling hair in the form of a wig.

Thanks to my hair transformation, I've recently made a few stunning, everyone-stop-and-look entrances. When it happens, the scalp below the synthetic cap tickles and I grin mischievously. Because I know what's really under the makeover: a head that is nearly bald from chemotherapy and a breast that's smaller than the other from a segmental mastectomy. But when I don my wig, the world doesn't see me as a pitiable cancer patient; I'm a sex goddess.

It even happened at the grocery store. I was wearing my rock star wig, the long, straight, dark brown one that's cut in layers and highlighted. As I sauntered through the store, beginning with the fresh fruits and vegetables and onto the freezer section, I occasionally swept the layered strands out of my face.

My appetite had been poor, and a friend suggested I try frozen ravioli for an easy meal with some protein. While I searched through frozen juices and breads, I pushed my cart past a man who was busily stocking the grocery freezers. He wasn't too busy to notice me. I continued searching the frozen vegetables and dinners, but could find no ravioli. So I returned to the beginning of the aisle to look again, passing the freezer fill-up man a second time.

"Can I help you with something?" he asked. Near my age, he was a nice-looking fellow with a smile topped with a mustache.

"I'm looking for frozen ravioli."

He searched a couple of cases and found it. He knew his way around the freezer section. "Is this what you want?" he asked as he held up the package.

I smiled. "That's it. Thank you."

He nodded and went back to his stacking tray. At least his body did; I could feel his eyes on me.

"Nice day, isn't it?" he said.

"It's a beautiful day."

"Have a good one," he said.

"You, too."

As I strolled away, my confidence buoyed and my head held high, I remembered all the times I had gone into the grocery store as a single woman. People said it was an excellent place to meet men, yet I continually left the store unnoticed. But I was no longer single. Nor was I interested in a date. Nonetheless, it was empowering to know the conversation could have gone farther. And there was laughter in my heart as I turned up the next aisle, thinking how I had never gotten that much attention in a grocery store, even when I was twenty years younger and twenty pounds lighter. The change in dynamics had to be a direct result of my long, silky tresses.

I finished filling my cart and proceeded to the checkout, where a woman in her early twenties started to ring up my items. Her eyes strayed from the bread to my head. "You have the most beautiful hair."

I have a compulsion toward total honesty. I fleetingly considered telling her it was a wig. But that would demand explaining the breast cancer, which would lead to some words about chemo. And what if the freezer fill-up man happened to walk by at that time?

So I smiled at the clerk. "Thank you."

She didn't really need to know I was bald underneath.

It's a crazy experience to be going through chemotherapy for breast cancer and have people looking at you like you've just arrived from Hollywood. That's how I feel when I pull on Butterscotch Blondie, my favorite wig. I knew as soon as I tried it on that I loved the way it made me look, but I didn't have the guts to buy it. Even buying a brunette wig that was so different from my previously God-given hair seemed extreme to me. Going blonde, well, it just seemed too far out.

But my friends Joan and Rebecca were with me, and they must have seen the same thing I did. About a week after our wig-shopping expedition, a third friend, Cindy, showed up at my door with a grin stretched across her face. I was just home from chemotherapy, so I didn't have quite all of my wits about me, but I was happy for a visitor, especially a visitor handing me a beautifully wrapped birthday gift.

I opened the card first. It said: "We each interviewed twelve blondes. They each told us (assured us) that blondes definitely have more fun. We want your opinion next. Have fun!" It was signed "Joan, Rebecca, Cindy, Tammy, Martha, and Deb."

I ripped into it. I lifted the top off the box, and there it was—Butterscotch Blondie.

"How did you know?"

She smiled and shrugged.

"I have to try it on for you."

So I raced into my bedroom to fit it on my head. Maybe I was half-delirious from the drugs coursing through my system, but when I looked in the mirror, I thought I was stunning.

I returned to the kitchen, my grin as wide as Cindy's. Her mouth dropped open as she looked at me. "You look like Heather Locklear! You look so much younger. And it brings out your eyes!"

Maybe, I thought, I had finally found a way to make a va-va-voom entrance.

When my husband, Jim, and I (as Butterscotch Blondie) walked into church on Sunday, tongues began to wag. Not more than a hundred people attend our church services, and Jim and I usually sit in the third row from the front. So everyone had a chance to see Jim sitting next to "that blonde woman"—that hussy who was taking advantage of poor Beth's illness and moving in on her husband. Ha! As if Jim would do such a thing, much less advertise it in front of our church family.

"I thought maybe you were your sister." (I don't have a sister.)

"I didn't recognize you at all."

"You look beautiful."

"You should wear it all the time."

"You look hot." (That was whispered into my ear.)

Most of the comments came from the men.

My husband prefers the rock star wig, because he favors brunettes, but after he heard from all of the men at church, he recognized the beauty of the blonde. And I knew that if I wanted to make an entrance, I could.

While people tell me I'm "hot" and ask if agents from Hollywood have been calling, I subsist on applesauce and Jell-O. The chemo plays horrid tricks with my taste buds, and I long for the day when a chocolate bar with almonds actually sounds appealing.

Some days, my wigs sit on their stands, and I wear my fuzzy, blue crocheted cap or my rainbow-colored fleece hat. Or I choose a purple or red bandana, which always make me look like a pirate. If it's warm enough, I go bald and revel in the freedom of it.

After my surgery, I wasn't thinking about hats or wigs. In the midst of researching cancer treatments, going for tests, and meeting with doctors, I had neither the time nor energy to think about how I looked. I was appreciating every minute I breathed, every ray of sunshine that graced the day, each look of love my husband sent in my direction. My heart and soul opened their tender spaces to receive the encouragement, support, and prayers that people shared. My life beneath, my life inside, was rich with emotion and experience, and that sustained and strengthened me in preparation for what was to come.

I could say this experience has transformed me inside and that this internal transformation now shows on the outside. Maybe that's why people look at me like they haven't before. I would like to think that when we are filled with appreciation for life and with gratitude for the love people show us, those feelings radiate through to our external selves.

Of course, I'm well aware of how important physical appearance is in our society.

But I'm also an optimist. I believe in the power of positive thinking and that laughter can ease the pain. While all of this hoopla about my hair makes me question the way what's on the surface tends to sway people, it also makes me smile and giggle. Surely, that's part of the healing process too.

—*Beth Dotson Brown*

Daffodils and Me

As a high school English teacher, I begin each school year with active lessons and immediate responsibility. My freshmen, eager and shy, respond to my idea of improvisation by presenting scenes from their summer reading. My juniors, reserved and curious, share "me-bags," each containing at least five important items from their lives. I participate too: a photo of my family, a book I've been reading, a small sculptured bicycle, my journal, and my Scrabble set. My journalism students divide into groups and brainstorm articles for the first issue of the school newspaper.

Before long, my classes and I begin to share a common breath. We move on to in-depth units. My freshmen read *Of Mice and Men*, and we put George Milton on trial for the death of Lennie Small. My juniors study immigration by creating family trees, sharing ethnic foods, and reading selections from

The Jungle. My journalism classes conduct interviews and gather opinions, take pictures and write articles.

Like a fruit smoothie—satisfying flavors, easy to digest—September blends into October. The autumn faces of my students emerge: scarlet brilliance from the sturdy oaks, steadfast-emerald from the evergreens, yellow-sunshine from the maples, and russet-blends from the sycamores. I feel like an American elm, hardy and hale . . . unaware that my leaves are about to fall and scatter.

January crashes into me with the force of an avalanche.

The doctors say I have breast cancer; I need surgery to remove the tumor, then chemotherapy, followed by radiation. My breath freezes; ice seeps into my lungs. My students listen with winter faces as I explain how I found the lump, met with a surgeon and then an oncologist, and planned a course of action. I'll be out for a few weeks, I tell them, and when I return, I may not look the same. I try to reassure them while bolstering myself against the unknown. The mighty tree is shorn of its leaves and shivers in the cold, but is not alone. Cards and letters, flowers and food flow into my home, warming me and helping to melt my fear.

On the first day of spring, the daffodils arrive. Proud green stems sprout yellow trumpets, which blossom and cheer me on. But I notice as they die that they cry yellow on my kitchen counter. And when I throw them away their stems snap hollow. I think about daffodils, the American Cancer Society's symbol of hope; then I think about being hollow. The surgeon hollowed out a portion of my breast. Nothing remained, and I hope that is true. I wonder about that place, that empty space in my chest. Music is made through hollow instruments. And a squirrel finds refuge in a hollow. When we see two majestic mountains and the land between, that, too, is a hollow, a place of peace and safety. I think about the cards I have received and the kindnesses bestowed, the phone calls and the e-mails and the visits and the poetry. And I know that my hollow is being refilled with music and bells and chocolate and chimes.

An oxymoron: April and chemotherapy. When I am able, I go into school and work with my students. Spring faces: sun-nurtured and nature-kissed. Their energy channels through my veins, displacing the Cytoxan and the Adriamycin that have infiltrated my body. Like a budding tree, I awaken to new life. Amazed, I smile through my day, thankful to feel complete and whole, a part of something grand. The compassion of my students and colleagues sustains me through June.

"I admire your courage and ability to face each day with a positive attitude," my student Suzi writes.

"You have taught me so much, not just grammar and literature, but to have a strong will and always try my hardest," writes Sara.

Greg says, "I've learned to stay strong and tough through every challenge in life and never give up."

In July, I receive radiation. To keep my positive energies flowing, I learn pranayama, a breathing exercise. I practice until prana (power) fills my body. I feel my chest expand and my world enlarge. I slow down and live through each breath, not because of each breath.

August I claim as mine. My treatments have ended, and school is weeks away. I surround myself with those who share my joy: my husband, my children, my family, my friends. I attend a writing retreat, where a colleague includes me in her poem: "You are what life is about and life renewed." I throw off my scarves and my wig and dive bald-headed into Duxbury Bay, then sit invigorated on a dock and watch the sun tease the water. Pedaling down unpaved paths and up steep hills, I explore Block Island by bike from the Mohegan Cliffs to the Northern Light. I spend a fortnight at the ocean. Strolling the crescent beach, I write my fears in the sand and see them sweep out to sea. Soon, I will reimmerse myself into school, but for now the air breathes through me, and I turn my face up to the sky.

Five years have passed, and I remain strong. My chest X-ray no longer reveals scar tissue. My blood is not anemic, and my platelets range is normal. Even though my breast looks as if maniacal scissors have ravaged it, it is still a part of me. My scar jags deep along my cleavage, so I can no longer wear low-cut dresses, bathing suits, or tank tops. Perhaps, as time goes by, I might consider the assaulted area as dimpled. But I must be grateful. A decade ago, my breast would have been lopped off. Years from now, a laser beam will have pinpointed the aberrant cells and destroyed them.

My right arm still tingles from the operation that removed and tested nineteen lymph nodes (all negative), so I do weight-bearing exercises to increase muscle mass. When I bike or work out, I wear padded gloves to absorb the pain. What's amazing to me is how many people poke or stroke my arm, just matter-of-factly. I've learned to endure that joy-buzzer vibration without jumping out of my skin.

I also remember to breathe. Like when I'm twelfth in line at a traffic light, or when a student asks for a bathroom pass at a critical point in class discussion, or when I've shared my thoughts and received hard-to-swallow criticism.

At first, my hair grew back dark and curly. When it was at the crew-cut stage, I rue that I didn't have the wherewithal to streak it pink or spike it yellow. Perhaps, as my sister-in-law Donna says, I was preoccupied.

Taste has taken its time to resume. My favorites, Junior Mints, so creamy and smooth, make me gag—even when I see the box. Tuna fish, once a necessity, causes nausea. "Discomfort foods" are what I call them now.

Many students who saw me through my ordeal still keep in touch. Whenever I see them, their faces smile as if their team had won the football game or their dance company had scored gold. They are thankful that I am alive (as am I), and every time Kevin or Mike or Zach chats with me about his future plans or one of my sweet coterie of girls shares her goals and dreams, I am infused with youthful energy.

My family and friends both forget and remember. They, too, have met mountains and have climbed them or tumbled and slid, fallen and soared.

Last September, I bought one hundred daffodils from the garden club and planted seventy-five (twenty-five wait in reserve). Today, they line my picture window, surround my mailbox, and like Jericho, trumpet proudly around my yard. When I walk among them, I hear their birth song, how they struggled upward, mixing with the earth, connecting with the air, gulping life, then emerging whole.

After six years pass, I participate in the three-day Susan G. Komen Walk for the Cure, bringing closure to a difficult period in my personal journey. I am thrilled to be walking, even if my body suffers some trauma. What are a few toenails and sore feet after having lost my hair and my eyelashes, not to mention a large portion of cherished flesh? It is a reminder that cancer touches all of us, at the most unlikely of times, and we must move past it.

When a florist handed out daffodils recently, I accepted one. And to my astonishment I said out loud, "Thank you. I am a cancer survivor." I have preserved that flower. Every day it reminds me of who I am, where I have been, and where I am going. "Ruth," it says. "*Carpe diem!* Seize the day! Stay alert, live determined, be stout."

My hollows have filled with hope and light, and I have become a daffodil woman.

—*Ruth Ellen Weiner*

A Breast Party

The first of my girlfriends arrived in a sheer nude bra, the next in a black lace camisole. I answered the door in a volcano-red push-up bra, and soon, nine of my dearest women friends were sitting around my table for a potluck feast—all of us in various stages of toplessness. So what exactly was going on in this respectable home in the suburbs of Boston?

A year earlier, after I had tossed a white lily down the abyss of my mother's grave, I started battling my health insurance company and my doctors for the privilege of a mammogram only six months after my last one. Images of my mother's face emboldened me: The dread in her eyes on her first day of chemo when a stately woman, bald as a peeled potato, strode through the waiting room; the way she gazed out her bedroom window at the vast blue sky, her final vision of this world. My mother had been six months late for her mammogram. A lot can happen in six months, I kept thinking.

One mammogram per year was what the managed healthcare enterprise had dictated for me. Two, they claimed, were not necessary, not cost-effective, and too much radiation. My primary care doctor, an oncologist, and a breast surgeon all refused to submit my requests for a second mammogram that year, but I didn't capitulate. By month nine, I had found a new primary care physician who said "yes" to the mammogram, and she conquered the layers of bureaucratic work to ensure it.

Luckily, almost every woman in America knows what it feels like to endure the squeezing of her breasts between cold, flattening, metal plates and to then sit in a scant hospital gown and wait for the verdict—wondering, *Will this be the year the bullet picks me off, or will I escape the merciless epidemic once again?* In the face of a serious medical history, which included lymph cancer, brain surgery, twisted intestines, and nerve pain, and had brought me perilously close to the Big Adios more than once, I had developed a perspective on bad news. It went something like this: Bad news will find its way to my front door soon enough, but I am not opening that door until it knocks. Having survived enough knocks, I had already discovered that divesting myself of the pre-worry worry makes no difference to the outcome. By age fifty-one, wrapped in a dusty rose gown, chilled, and goose-bumped, I had already acquired an instinct for declining much of the misery that is plentiful during miserable times. So I sat in the oh-so-soothing waiting room, filing the same fingernail into oblivion and eyeing the lady with the clipboard as she handed out our life sentences. One woman left crying; two escaped. There were two options in this breast center: the you're-safe huddle or the come-with-me signal. Then The Clipboard hooked me with her *gotcha* eyes and waved me into her little room. She didn't need to say a word.

I spent the rest of the day rehearsing my final moments and grieving for my son's motherless future. But by sunset, I had decided that his mother would live. My own wait-to-worry theory had clicked in. I refused to suffer until *after* the biopsy, I told my son over the phone that night, and together we exercised our optimism option. For a full seven days, we attributed benevolence to the suspicious cluster of calcium deposits.

On the evening the surgeon called with the biopsy results, my son was home from college. "It wasn't what we would have wanted" was how the surgeon worded it. Then she suggested that I get both breasts lopped off, as if they were a couple of warts.

Quickly, before the full impact set in, I prayed for an attitude strategy, and that is when my dead mother came forward with one of her best inspirations. Upon hanging up with the surgeon, I repeated it to my son: "If we have a choice between making this a bigger drama or a smaller drama, let's make it a smaller drama." He breathed relief.

In the midst of my smaller drama program, I liberated several wildly productive primal cries while still managing an efficient cancer central switchboard from my home office. I interviewed eleven doctors in New York, Boston, and Los Angeles, and sorted through the tangle of their opposing opinions. What compelled me were these memories: how thrilled my mother had been when "the doctor said" he could save her breast . . . and how, when she'd died, she died with that breast.

So, my decision made, I set off window-shopping for new breasts at my health club, assessing size and shape—young, old, full, perky, pointy—constructing a profile of what I wanted my two reconstructed breasts to look like. I stopped short of asking a complete stranger in the sauna what her bra size might be, but just barely. Then, a week before the bilateral mastectomy, reaching for something to up-shift me into a positive emotional position, I threw a topless-optional party with my friends. We came together to send off my "girls" before they were snatched from me.

After dinner, my friends surrounded me on the couch, and we told breast stories. We talked about stuffing our teenage bras, first feels in summer camp, and the functional days, when we swelled with milk for our babies. The friend with the beautiful voice sang, the poet read, the psychiatrist held my right hand and the psychologist the left, the theatre director led a meditation, and the photographer friend mostly forgot to take photos. We massaged backs, stroked arms, laughed, hugged, and prayed for health. At one point, I pulled up my red bra and said, "Aren't they beautiful!" Before the night ended, we stood in a close huddle, and each friend visualized me after the surgery: "I see you swimming and strong." . . . "I see you and your son on a plane for Bali." . . . "I see you in a polka dot bikini."

This is what I can tell you about the dreaded, supposedly horrible, bilateral mastectomy: I never felt like I lost my breasts. After the eleven-hour, three-surgeon operation, I just woke up with new breasts. As a bonus, because my new breasts were formed from the fat of another region of my body, I was blessed with a new and improved look overall. I turned out to be one of the lucky ones, knock on wood, whose cancer cells did not travel into her lymph nodes and who caught the cancer early with a mammogram (enough said). The prognosis is positive. The baddest of bad news did not find me.

No matter the prospects, in the cruelest of days, in the darkest of dark, inspiration abounds. For every woman who has waited in a hospital gown for the verdict and for every woman within reach of Fear, Pain, and Suffering, the monsters of this epidemic, I offer the seemingly paradoxical idea of a breast party, topless or not, as a life-affirming ritual of support, as a shared celebration of our beauty and our strength.

—Donna Conrad

The Power of Knowledge

My mother had a secret. I knew she didn't want to tell me it until after the holiday. My in-laws were driving down from Pennsylvania to spend Easter with our family in North Carolina, and my mother didn't want to ruin their visit.

The phone call from New York came the afternoon after my in-laws left.

"Do you have five minutes?"

I can usually tell by the tone of my mother's voice if she has good news or bad, and this time I knew it was going to be bad news. I'm experienced with receiving this kind of news.

The first time bad news came was when I was ten. My mother had breast cancer in her left breast. The second time was in my twenties. That was the when my mother had breast cancer in her right breast. And then when I was in my thirties, she had ovarian cancer.

I looked at my children who were playing quietly on the floor and sat down on the couch. "Sure, I have five minutes." I put the phone to my other ear. "You got the test results back, didn't you?"

Not that the results would be a surprise. When I had talked to her about getting the genetic testing done, she said the same thing we always said about breast cancer: It ran in our family. As I did some reading, I found out that I needed to know more than what my family tree told me. I needed to know whether there was a genetic reason for our breast cancer, so that, if there was, we could consider myriad other options.

There was a brief pause.

"I knew you got the results of the genetic testing back and weren't telling me," I said with a nervous laugh.

We always joke that my mother has ESP. Sometimes I think I'm gaining this ability, along with many other traits that I seem to share with my mother. There are our German noses and thick hair and our propensity to call things by the wrong name and to confuse our holidays, but we would both agree that there is one way in which I don't want to be like my mother.

"I have the BRCA1 gene mutation."

The words came across the phone, and time stood still for several seconds.

The results meant that breast cancer officially ran in our family. A woman's lifetime risk for developing breast and/or ovarian cancer is significantly higher than the general population if she has the BRCA1 mutation. The literature my mother was provided by the testing facility stated that mutation carriers have a 33 to 50 percent chance of developing breast cancer by age fifty, whereas noncarriers have a 2 percent chance, and a 27 to 44 percent chance of developing ovarian cancer by age seventy, while noncarriers have less than a 2 percent chance. My family's experiences with breast cancer all began in their late thirties and early forties.

The news would take a few days to settle in, but for now I was surprisingly relieved. So much of the past now made sense, especially my mother having first developed breast cancer at only forty years old.

"Are you okay?" asked my mother.

"We expected this, right?" I said.

The limbs of my family tree are heavy with women who have had breast cancer, including three family members—my mother's grandmother, cousin, and sister—who all died from it in their early forties.

"It's good we know," I said. "We needed to know."

Now, the women in my family could plan for their futures with this information. I felt powerful knowing that we had identified the enemy and could now focus on fighting this disease earlier than we had in the past.

My doctors always told me to get serious about breast cancer when I was ten years younger than my mother when she was first diagnosed, and the time had come. For the past few months, I had been to appointments at the high-risk breast cancer clinic, with the genetic counselor and the gynecological oncologist. I started keeping a folder of information and business cards, so I could make sense of all of the specialists I had seen. When I gave my family history, the doctor's eyes always got bigger. And now it seemed we had discovered the crown jewel of it all—a genetic explanation. Just that morning, hours before my mother's enlightening call, I had been to the oncologist to talk about screening for ovarian cancer.

"The doctor asked me if anyone else in our family had ovarian cancer," I said to Mom. "I told him that most everyone who got breast cancer in our family died in their forties. So they could have gotten it when they got older, . . ."

"But I survived," my mother completed my thought.

Somehow, through all of our family experiences with cancer, death had never even seemed like an option for my mother. Sure, there were always "those moments" when it all seemed overwhelming. I'm sure in the privacy of her mind, in the silence of a hospital room late at night, or when chemotherapy took its toll, my mother thought about not making it through cancer, but she never said it to me. Until the doctor had asked me the question that morning, I never considered what the other outcome could have been over the years.

My mother has always said that her sister saved her life. When my aunt discovered she had a lump in her breast, there was no genetic test to tell her this was a ticking time-bomb in her body. It was the 1980s, and doctors didn't seem to push to followup on lumps as much then as they do now. My aunt was told to wait and see. My mother found the first lump in her own breast when my aunt was dying from metastatic breast cancer. There was no waiting to follow up on my mother's lump, and early diagnosis saved her life.

I have made my own appointment to see if I, too, carry the gene mutation. It's tomorrow. They'll draw some blood and send it off to a laboratory. There's a 50 percent chance I inherited the gene. I'm not sure when the results will come, but I do know it will mark a huge point in my life.

"Are you worried?" asked my mother on our call tonight.

"Yes, a little."

I've already read too much literature and lived through my mother's cancer, so I knew what came along with having the gene.

"There's no use in worrying until you know," she said.

I smiled. My mother was a self-professed worrier about anything and everything.

"It will be fine either way," I said.

"Yes, it will."

My mother survived cancer three times. I can't imagine my life without her. My childhood self would have sorely missed her, and my adult life would have had an empty space. We have our usual disagreements, but she has been there for my graduation, my wedding, my babies' births and sicknesses, and for hundreds of phone calls about nothing in particular.

My cousin says she thinks of her mother every day.

Genetic testing has given us something we never had before: a chance at beating breast cancer before it even begins. Thank you, Aunt Sharon. You saved my mother's life. And thank you, Mom, for giving the future generations of our family a better chance at beating this disease. Now we know.

—*Janine Boldrin*

Go Ahead and Wish for It

I stood in the examining room with a lump in my breast that felt big enough to eat my life, leaned against my husband's chest, and blurted, "I want to be here to see how it all turns out."

"It" was the story of our life, of course, especially the chapter called "The Future" that belonged to our three kids—fourteen, eleven, and not quite nine years old. Watching them grow had been the most fun I'd ever had, and it only got better each year. I was fascinated by the things they noticed and the things they ignored, by the foods they ate or shunned, by the different ways they found to play with the same toy. They were alike but so different that I gained a new respect for genes.

My three children were individuals to me right from the start. The first was a night person, the second a morning person, and the last one needed hardly any sleep at all. Two took to the water like fish; the other was a more reluctant swimmer. The first was a determined force to be reckoned with, the second a lucky soul who thrilled to the big themes of good versus evil in epic movies, and the third had an offbeat sense of humor and insight that pushed him into the creative class.

The possibility that I might not be here to see what kind of adults they became drove me wild. The mammogram was negative, but the doctor wasn't satisfied. The needle biopsy was inconclusive. The surgical biopsy, though, came back loud and clear: malignant.

At forty-one, I had breast cancer—ductal carcinoma, stage two. My mother had survived breast cancer in both breasts—but after menopause. My treatment would have to allow for estrogen still coursing through my body. I had one mastectomy, and then a year later a second, even though my cancer was only in one breast. It was only a matter of time, the doctors said. Between surgeries, the oncologist recommended aggressive chemotherapy; the cancer was streaming. I agreed. I would do whatever it took to increase the chances that I would be there to see what happened. The kids were characters in my life—living, changing human beings—and anything was possible.

So we all five struggled through six monthly chemo treatments that left me exhausted, emotionally fragile, and lacking perspective. And did I say exhausted? "Chemo-tired" became the new phrase in our house. It came with huge black circles under my eyes, a brain that refused to wrap around facts for hours every day, and limbs that just had no oomph. By early evening, I was drained of all energy.

The kids learned to help. The oldest was good at reality checks. She wouldn't accept excuses or self-pity. The two youngest learned how to be sensitive and to tote and hoist things I simply couldn't. They got used to serious conversations at the dinner table about what was really important in life. All three learned to remind me of my wig when I started to dash out without it. Their dad organized bed-making and sheet-washing every Saturday, teaching them how to make their own beds. There was a new reality in our house.

Men married to women with breast cancer can rise to the occasion, developing nurturing skills no one knew they had. They become super husbands. This happened in our house. My husband became nurse, chauffeur, patient listener, researcher, cheerleader, grocery shopper, and chief mood lifter. He listened and talked me through all the treatments and all the fears. His patience grew by leaps and bounds.

Three kids watched this happen in front of their eyes. Dad took care of Mom, no questions asked. He also took care of them and the house.

For my part, I cut back at work, took a loss in salary, and focused on realigning my priorities. If I couldn't do it all, I would have to choose. Work was just work, and children came first. I learned to say no.

At the end of the first year, the doctor said the magic words, "You are a survivor." I hadn't allowed myself to think that. I was convinced that if I presumed too much, fate would strike me down.

By then, I had started a five-year course of tamoxifen, which alternately made me rage impotently at things I couldn't change and fear ordinary things, such as freeway-driving in urban areas. It is one powerful drug. It bonds with estrogen so cancer cells can't, depriving them of food, but it can cause cruel hormonal swings.

Another year went by and another. The bone scans were negative. The chest X-rays were negative. No lumps popped up, despite my anxious fingers looking for them everywhere, even on my forehead. We learned to celebrate the ordinariness of everyday life—school activities, family vacations, and most of all, dinner. By the time other families had burned out on dinner or given up in the face of sports practices, we got our second wind. At the dinner table, everybody had a place, a say, and an audience. The food was not as important as the conversation and the company. We laughed and told the best thing that happened to us that day over meals only partially made from scratch. We lingered, reluctant to leave the circle of five that fed our souls as well as our bodies.

Then, big changes started. Our daughter graduated from high school. We celebrated by taking all three kids on a cruise to Alaska. Soon after, our oldest son graduated. We celebrated by taking all three kids to England and Ireland. Then our youngest, not quite nine when I was diagnosed with cancer, graduated from high school. We celebrated by taking everyone on a Caribbean cruise.

How could we do this? I went back to work fulltime. We stayed in our smallish house. We gave up the idea of a summer cottage or even a boat. We declined to buy our high school children cars or TVs for their rooms. We joined no private clubs. We made choices more mindfully than I ever would have imagined. Our money was for college and time together as a family.

Soon, eagerly, I began to glimpse that chapter called "The Future" in the choices the kids made, especially when it came to college. They all went to the University of Michigan, only an hour from our home, but they chose individual paths that crossed only at football or hockey games. They were in different degree programs. I watched in awe as one succeeded in stand-up comedy, as one rose to leadership in the university's marching band, and as one edited articles in the *Michigan Daily*. They had unique skills and unique strengths that made life on summer vacations very sweet. They could take over, one at a time, and solve different problems, suggest different solutions, and come up with creative ways to spend a weekend. When the five of us were together, nothing could sink us. Did coping with a mother who had cancer while they were young have any effect on their problem-solving abilities? We'll never know.

The college graduations started, followed by the professional school graduations. We never took one for granted. At each, we had much to cheer, much to be grateful for, and much to remember. This, I would tell myself, is what I wanted to see all those years ago when they told me I had cancer. This is why I went through not only a bilateral mastectomy but aggressive chemotherapy as well. I wanted to be at my children's graduations. And I was.

The characters in my life, those who started out as the world's most fascinating babies (at least to me), have become a doctor, a lawyer, and a computer engineer. They are even more fascinating now (not just to me).

In my case, we beat cancer by sticking to the treatment recommended by top-notch medical people and with something else—group dynamics. We leaned on each other and grew stronger doing so. Cancer became a factor in our lives, just like where we live and where we work. It came with pluses and minuses, and we—as a group of five—worked not to let the minuses sink us. We tried to accept cancer as part of the background noise, and then ignore it. Most of all, we learned to think about what we really want to do and how to do it.

When I wished to see how the story came out, I hit the jackpot. Wishes do come true.

So I've made a new wish. It's to be here if any grandchildren show up. I have a lot of stories I want to tell them.

—*Sheila O'Brien Schimpf*

Like a Rock

It had been almost a year since I had been diag-nosed with breast cancer. As I glanced at my kitchen calendar, teaming with plans and commit-ments, the date seemed to jump out at me. That square seemed larger than any of the others on the page. The number seemed to pulsate.

The previous spring, after navigating the holi-days, wet weather, surgeries, and two months of daily radiation, I was tired. I felt depleted. Vulner-able. I noticed I felt more comfortable curled up in bed with a book or watching television than visit-ing with people. I no longer knew the art of mak-ing small talk.

After the rainy season ended, our daughter, Kira's, class at school began organizing its spring camping trip to Yosemite. My husband, Michael, volunteered to go along. They would be gone a week. I could spend some time by myself. They could spend some time away from me. We would all benefit.

I had never been to Yosemite. I was born and raised in Northern California, but somehow never made the trip. Images of crowds always put me off. Camping has never been one of my favorite pastimes. But at the end of the week when they got home with their stories and their rolls of film, I was envious.

"Call the Wawona," said Michael. "Get us a reservation for a long weekend. You'll love it."

The first available opening wouldn't be for five months. I grabbed it. Put it on the calendar and went on about my business.

Our Yosemite weekend finally arrived. We packed up the car. Dropped Kira off at her friend Katy's. Took the dog to the kennel, and we were off.

This would be our first weekend alone since I had gotten sick. We didn't even turn on the radio. We talked. We gazed out the windows. We stopped for coffee and apricot scones. It didn't matter where we were going or if we ever got there. It was simply grand to be on the road.

I watched as the landscape changed from valley to foothills. I smelled the pines as we climbed in elevation. We wound along the Merced River. A lone fisherman stood under the shade of an oak, casting his line. As we entered the park, I was amazed at the fall colors. The deep crimson and burnished golds of the dogwoods and birch. The indigo sky. And around the bend, the cool granite of El Capitan.

I was beginning to get it.

"Wait," Michael kept telling me, "there's more."

We drove through the valley and back out again, heading toward Wawona. A sign on the left read: "Glacier Point, 16 miles." We turned off and drove through the woods. The air was as crisp as fall apples.

I was unprepared. Nothing anyone could have said would have been adequate. As we came around the corner, there it was: Half Dome.

We pulled off the road and parked. There was a small clearing and an outcropping of rocks. Michael and I climbed out onto the smooth granite ledge. It was so beautiful I had to remind myself to breathe.

The sun was shining on the back side of the dome, highlighting the smooth, round curve. The face was in shadow, accentuating its cold, flat surface.

The valley lay before us. The deep gouge where the glacier cut its path was just to the left. But my gaze kept returning to the huge granite monument. As the sun rotated, light began to pour over the sheared-off portion of the dome, exposing the crevices. The web of scars. Imperfections that add to the beauty. That tell a story.

I leaned back against Michael and experienced a perfect moment in time. After everything—floods, storms, avalanches, and glaciers—Half Dome is still here.

And so am I.

—*Claudia Sternbach*

Contributors

Petrina Aubol ("The Challenge"), a Syracuse University journalism graduate, always wanted to write, but only after her bout with cancer did she leave the radio business and hit the keyboard. A former New Yorker, she now gets inspiration from grazing milk cows in rural Tennessee, where she lives with husband, Dean, and fifteen-year-old spaniel, Herman.

C. Lynn Beck ("Dancing in the Moonlight") is a freelance author living in Utah. She and her mom, Roberta Kieliger, co-design breast cancer-themed greeting cards for an online store; a portion of the proceeds go to the Susan G. Komen for the Cure® foundation.

Janine Boldrin ("The Power of Knowledge") is a writer who lives in West Point, New York, with her husband and two sons. Soon after writing this essay, Janine found out that she does carry the same BRCA1 genetic mutation as her mother. For more information about hereditary breast and ovarian cancer, visit *www.facingourrisk.org.*

Annette M. Bower ("Good to Go"), of Regina, Saskatchewan, Canada, is a breast cancer survivor since 2001. A freelance writer, she is proud to also be published in *A Cup of Comfort® for Mothers and Sons.*

Beth Dotson Brown ("The Hoopla about Hair") is a freelance writer, editor, and mentor who lives in Lancaster, Kentucky. While going through cancer treatment, she wrote her first book, *Yes! I Am Catholic,* published by St. Mary's Press. Beth continues to write and no longer attracts special attention now that her natural hair has returned.

Christy Caballero ("Warrior Women Wear Pink") lives a few deer trails off the beaten path in Oregon, with the trees, wildlife, and pets she loves so much. Her work has appeared in numerous *Cup of Comfort®* books as well as in other anthologies. She has received national journalism awards and a Maxwell award from the Dog Writers Association of America.

Joan A. Cody ("Timing Is Everything") is a published author who lives in Massachusetts with her husband of fifty-three years. She spends her spare time with her six children and eighteen grandchildren.

Karen A. Condon ("Letter 7") is a fiction writer from Springfield, Massachusetts. She has an MFA from the University of Massachusetts in Amherst, and works with deaf students at area colleges. The author of *Are You a Survivor?*, a collection of short stories dealing with cancer treatment, she is currently working on a novel.

Donna Conrad ("A Breast Party") is a writer and editor who resides in Boston and Los Angeles. Her children's book, *See You Soon Moon*, has won several awards, and her short stories and essays appear frequently in literary journals. The founder of College Bound Essays, she helps students discover and craft their college essays.

Margaret B. Davidson ("Remember Only the Laughter") lives with her husband in upstate New York. Retired from regular employment, Margaret enjoys visiting her children and grandchildren, writing flash fiction, and playing golf, tennis, and the occasional game of bridge. More than two years after her surgery, she remains cancer-free.

Michele Ivy Davis ("Bonus Time") lives in Florida, where she has become a freelance writer specializing in articles for police, fire rescue, and emergency medical service (EMS) magazines. After her cancer diagnosis, she also wrote her first novel, *Evangeline Brown and the Cadillac Motel*, which has won national and international awards.

Stacia Deutsch ("Lessons from the Chemo Room") is a children's author living in Irvine, California, with her three children. In addition to their own creative series, Stacia and her coauthor have also written nonfiction texts, a young adult comedy, mysteries, and junior movie tie-in novels for summer blockbuster films. Chemo saved Stacia's life; writing saved her soul.

Glen Finland ("Missing Parts") lives in McLean, Virginia, and teaches writing at American University. This story is part of her collection, *The Inside of an Egg.* Her work has also appeared in the *Washington Post, American Magazine, Revolution,* and the *East Coast Women's Anthology.* She is the recipient of the Southeastern Writers Best Fiction award.

Lauren Reece Flaum ("Inga") is a native New Yorker who has spent the last twenty years living, writing, and raising her family in Iowa City, Iowa. She has published essays on school board governance, golf, and life with breast cancer and is the author of the play *The Boyhood Dreams of Marc Chagall.*

Harriett Ford ("Probably Nothing") is a reporter and advice/humor columnist for "Sara and Sadie's Sense and Nonsense," in the *Rockford Labor News.* She is a full-time grandmother and writer of short stories set in the Ozark hills of Missouri, where she and husband, John, own a home.

Sally Gilchrest-Unrau ("Location, Location, Location"), born in Stratford, Connecticut, presently resides in Morden, Manitoba, Canada. She graduated from Southern Connecticut State College with a bachelor of science in special education and worked in early childhood development until her recent retirement. She is married to Hank, and has a daughter, Michelle. Her passion is quilting.

Beth Gooch ("The Luckiest Family on the Block") is a copy editor at the *Commercial Appeal* newspaper in

Memphis, Tennessee. Her mother, Elizabeth Gooch, and her sister, Nancy Luke, both faced breast cancer with humor and optimism, teaching Beth that even the most difficult days bring something to smile about. But their courage in spite of problems also had another effect: Beth has no tolerance for whiners!

Kathleen Griswold ("From To-Do to Ta-Da!") lives in a suburb of Cleveland, Ohio, with her two Labrador retrievers. She is active in breast cancer awareness and hopes to eliminate the threat of breast cancer from the lives of her two wonderful daughters.

Caroline Castle Hicks ("Staying Afloat") is a freelance writer in North Carolina whose work has appeared in numerous national and regional publications. She is the author of a collection of essays, poems, and public radio commentary entitled *Such Stuff as Stars Are Made of: Thoughts on Savoring the Wonders in Everyday Life.*

Cathy Howard ("Only My Sisters Understand") lives in Grand Island, Nebraska. She teaches middle-school English at Central Catholic High School, where her husband, John, also teaches. The couple has two sons, Kenny and Tommy. She recently wrote a book about growing up with her ten brothers and sisters called *Our House.*

Jennifer D. Jenkins ("There's No Place Like Normal") is a native of southeast Louisiana, currently residing in Houma, a Cajun community near the Gulf of Mexico. An auditor by day, she spends her evenings relaxing with her husband, daughter, and a good book. This is her first, and only, bout with breast cancer.

Maria S. Judge ("I Went and Washed That Hair Right Offa My Head") was born in Germany, raised in Ireland, Chile, and Indiana, and now lives in the Boston area. She has written extensively about her childhood and travels with her parents and eight siblings. She works as director of administration at Physicians for Human Rights.

Kate Kenworthy ("Mind Over Cancer") is a coauthor of *The Everything® Guide to Being a Personal Trainer*. She is the head personal trainer at Edge Athletics Performance and Training Center in Lincoln, Rhode Island, and resides with her partner, Stephen, and daughter, Victoria, in Cumberland.

Sheryl Kraft ("The Friend Who Came and Went"), of Wilton, Connecticut, is a freelance writer specializing in health, fitness, and wellness. She holds a masters in nonfiction writing from Sarah Lawrence College. Her work has appeared in *JAMA*, *Weight Watchers*, *AARP*, *Bottom Line/Health*, *Caring Today*, and *Wilton Magazine*. She credits her husband, Alan, and sons Jonathan and Jeremy, for inspiring her to write.

Jennifer S. Kutzik ("Carrying My Head in a Nordstrom's Bag") lives in Fort Collins, Colorado. She earned a bachelor of arts degree from Purdue University and has served as a library professional at Colorado State University Libraries since 1973. Jennifer is a Reach to Recovery volunteer for the American Cancer Society. Her leisure activities include exercise, cooking, needlework, writing, and traveling with her husband.

Barbara Leedom ("Breast Cancer, Funny?"), of South Yarmouth, Massachusetts, is a retired English teacher and public relations writer. She lives on fragile Cape Cod, where she writes, tutors, and walks beaches.

Nikki Marchesiello ("Code Red") lives in Marin County, California. She works with her husband, Nino, in his vineyard equipment business, and with her son, a general building contractor. Nikki enjoys spending time with her family, walking her dog, reading, and writing. She is currently working on a collection of personal essays.

Rosalie Marsh-Boinus ("The Pebble and the Rock: A Love Story") is a native of St. Paul, Minnesota, currently residing in Laguna Beach, California, where she works with her husband creating television and movie scripts. A two-time survivor of breast cancer, she has found that healing comes from creating art, and the emotional battle of the disease is often a theme of her work.

Rachel Beth McClain ("Surviving Period") is a stay-at-home mom and a freelance writer currently living in Los Angeles, but she loves every new place the military sends her family. Married to an active-duty military member and a former active-duty military member herself, she left the service to raise her son and to more actively pursue her dream of writing. She's been published in several online magazines and is finishing her first young adult novel.

Alice Muschany ("Hidden Treasures") lives in Flint Hill, Missouri. She has been employed by MEMC for thirty-nine years, and she and her husband are looking forward to retirement. In addition to her hobbies of gardening, photography, and writing, her eight grandchildren provide lots of entertainment.

Mary Ann O'Rourke ("Proceed") lives in Barrington, Illinois, a suburb of Chicago, with her husband and two sons. A former corporate editor and public relations executive, she is currently a stay-at-home mom. She enjoys swimming, reading, and watching her sons grow up, and recently celebrated her fiftieth birthday skiing in Colorado with her college roommate and their families.

Joseph Pantatello ("The 'M' Word") is retired and has been writing for several years. His stories have been published in seven anthologies and have won awards in major writing competitions. He enjoys writing fantasy, mystery, and a little romance to please his wife, Caroline. He is a longtime member of the prestigious Long Island Writers' Guild and editor of the *The Write Stuff* newsletter.

Laura Walsh Plunkett ("My Third Lung") resides in Overland Park, Kansas, with her husband and two children. She studied journalism and English while completing her undergraduate and graduate degrees in business and is a writer, breast cancer advocate and avid road cyclist.

Kathie Ragsdale ("Filling Up and Spilling Over"), a writer and newspaper editor, lives in Chester, New Hampshire, with her husband, two dogs, a cat, and a bird. She cared for her previous husband as well as her mother while they battled fatal cancers. She still believes in miracles.

Linda Holland Rathkopf ("Survival of the Fittest") lives in Brooklyn Heights, New York. She is a fine artist, illustrator, and playwright. Her art has been in galleries across the northeastern United States, and her plays have been produced in California, Connecticut, Colorado, Kentucky, New York, and Vermont.

Allison Jean Roberts ("Never Say Never") resides in Barrie, Ontario, Canada, with her husband, Marty, and their two children, Tyler and Taryn. She is a customer service manager, an advocate for young women with breast cancer in her community, and has paddled for the past three years on an all-breast-cancer-survivor dragon boat team.

Jeanne Schambra ("Before and After") lives in Manorville, New York. She recently sold her house and is looking forward to traveling, writing her book, and bumming off her friends and family for a little while before she settles down in New Jersey with her new love. She thanks God every day for letting her see beauty in the "after."

Sheila O'Brien Schimpf ("Go Ahead and Wish for It") lives in East Lansing, Michigan, with her super husband and three golden retrievers. A former newspaper reporter and weekly columnist, she is now trying her hand at fiction and teaches journalism at Michigan State University some semesters. Her three children have jobs (with health insurance) on the East and the West Coasts, but they come home several times a year.

Anya Silver ("In the Eye of the Sparrow") is an English professor and poet who teaches at Mercer University in Macon, Georgia. She was diagnosed with inflammatory breast cancer in 2004. Her first book of poetry will be published by the Louisiana State University Press. She lives in Macon with her husband and son. Her essay in this book is dedicated to the memory of Juliet Jones and Deborah Tall.

Virginia Hardee Silverman ("Pieta's Promise") was born and raised in rural eastern North Carolina. A marketing executive with *Fortune* 100 companies for twenty-five years, she is currently senior vice president of marketing for Lindora Medical Weight Control. She recently completed her master of fine arts in creative nonfiction at Antioch University in Los Angeles, and is also a singer, cancer survivor, and mother of a nine-year-old daughter, Eve.

Claudia Sternbach ("Like a Rock") is a newspaper columnist and feature writer living in Aptos, California. The author of *Now Breathe* (Whiteaker Press), she recently completed her first novel.

Jennifer Swanson ("Well Wishes") lives and writes in Fort Lauderdale, Florida. She lives in the worlds of business and art, perhaps because her father was a research chemist and her mother a poet and social service worker. She began following her dreams and writing more extensively after being diagnosed with breast cancer in 2003. Her writing focuses on becoming whole in a place of brokenness.

Paula Sword ("Saving Grace"), a two-year breast cancer survivor, lost her mother to breast cancer twenty years ago. She credits her survival to an early start on mammograms, knowing her body through BSE, wonderful friends and family, and finding humor in life. A speech pathologist for twenty-five years, she lives in McDonough, Georgia, and enjoys riding her motorcycle to work. This is her second published story.

Susan B. Townsend ("Led by Love") is a writer and stay-at-home mother who lives in Virginia with her husband and five children. She is the author of *A Bouquet for Mother* and *A Bouquet for Grandmother* and is the co-editor of several Christian volumes in the *Cup of Comfort*® series.

Ruth Ellen Weiner ("Daffodils and Me"), a retired high school English teacher, is a journalist on staff at a newspaper south of Boston. A wife, mother, and grandmother, she enjoys spending time with her family. She reads avidly, bicycles globally, and writes passionately, and recently took up fencing through a program for cancer patients. Her stories have appeared in *We Teach Them All* and *Teaching Voices*. She won the New England Writers' Marjory Bartlett Singer Award for Short Fiction in 2007.

Julie A. Whitney ("Dear Tumor"), a breast cancer survivor from Westminster, Colorado, has been blessed with three amazing children, one adorable granddaughter, a supportive boyfriend, one precious puppy, and the world's greatest friends. She spent four years as an Air Force security police investigator and now works full-time as a registered nurse. A certified personal trainer who loves the outdoors, she can often be found running, biking, golfing, or simply enjoying the gifts that cancer left behind.

About the Editor

Colleen Sell has compiled and edited more than twenty-five volumes of the *Cup of Comfort®* book series. She has authored, ghostwritten, or edited numerous books; published scores of articles; and served as editor-in-chief of two award-winning consumer magazines. She and the love of her midlife, T. N. Trudeau, share a large extended family, a turn-of-the-century farmhouse that is perpetually under renovation, a forty-acre spread in the Pacific Northwest that is being slowly transformed into an organic blueberry and lavender farm, and a border collie mutt who watches over it all with amusement.

REDBOOK is the only magazine dedicated to your life—just as it is.

From health and home to beauty, fashion, love, money, and more, REDBOOK is packed with advice to keep your busy world moving, plus ideas to keep you connected to the part of your life for you alone.

WHAT READERS ARE SAYING:

"REDBOOK represents and celebrates every woman—those with careers and those who stay and home—and I would like to applaud you for doing such a beautiful job."

"Thank you, REDBOOK, for being there at the exact time I needed you, helping me get out of debt and, most of all, for reminding me of what is really important in life!"

REDBOOK IS ABOUT WHAT'S AT THE HEART OF YOUR LIFE: YOU!
VISIT ORDER.REDBOOKMAG.COM TO SUBSCRIBE NOW.

REDBOOK IS PROUD TO PARTNER WITH CUP OF COMFORT TO HELP THOSE AFFECTED BY BREAST CANCER SHARE THEIR STORIES OF COURAGE, INSPIRATION, AND LOVE.